Clive Phillipps-Wolley

Savage Svânetia

Vol. 1

Clive Phillipps-Wolley

Savage Svânetia
Vol. 1

ISBN/EAN: 9783337312527

Printed in Europe, USA, Canada, Australia, Japan

Cover: Foto ©ninafisch / pixelio.de

More available books at **www.hansebooks.com**

Frontispiece to Vol. 1.

VALLEY OF THE RION.

SAVAGE SVÂNETIA

BY

CLIVE PHILLIPPS-WOLLEY, F.R.G.S.

AUTHOR OF 'SPORT IN THE CRIMEA AND CAUCASUS'

IN TWO VOLUMES—VOL. I.

LONDON
RICHARD BENTLEY & SON, NEW BURLINGTON STREET
Publishers in Ordinary to Her Majesty the Queen
1883

TO
MY WIFE.

On a mist-hidden ridge of the mountain,
   Where the chamois and tûr live alone,
Lies a hunter who watches the fountain,
   And the stars watch that hunter, mine own!
There's just room for his rifle beside him,
   Just room for his guide at his feet;
Some two dozen inches divide him
   From death and eternity, sweet!
The mountain with grey hoary fingers
   Points up to the heaven above:
He kneels to his God first—then lingers,
   And wistfully dreams of his love.
The torrent that rages beneath him
   Just makes itself heard in a moan,
While the thunder-clouds stooping enwreath him
   And curtain his pillow of stone.
The lightning that gleams on his face, girl,
   Finds a smile born of thinking of thee;
And the storm wind that swept o'er the place, girl,
   Took a love message over the sea:
For soft grows the pillow of stone, dear,
   All the mountain with beauty is rife,
There is nothing for him to bemoan, dear,
   Who can trust in his God and his wife.

                              C. P.-W.

PREFACE.

In offering 'Savage Svânetia' to my readers I am acting upon the advice of one of the reviewers of my former book, 'Sport in the Crimea and Caucasus.'

He it was, who, writing in the 'Saturday Review,' first called my attention to Svânetia and the forest region of Lekêra as being among the least known corners of the Caucasus. Svânetia had always been spoken of to me as a hungry land inhabited by an angry people. The Russians themselves know very little of either the country or its inhabitants, and hence the exaggerated reports of the danger of travelling amongst them. An outline map of the country will be found on the cover of my book, and the best map published for the Government at Tiflis has been handed over by me to the Royal Geographical Society, to which I have the honour to belong, and there, no doubt, those anxious for a more intimate acquaintance with the topography of Svânetia would be allowed to see it.

That the Caucasus contains at the present moment an army of 130,000 men, for the maintenance of which there is but one obvious reason—that it is on the direct road from Russia to our Indian frontier; that an expensive line of rail has just been completed from Poti on the Black Sea to Baku on the Caspian, from the eastern shores of which the line may easily be extended to Herat, seem to me reasons for making every corner of the Caucasus interesting to Englishmen.

But it is not of the country in general as the great base for operations beyond the Caspian that I have written, since on such matters the unauthorised traveller is little likely to gain a hearing; but rather of the general aspect, people, and game of the least known corner of it. May this my second venture find as much favour in the eyes of my critics as did my first.

CLIVE PHILLIPPS-WOLLEY.

MORGAN HALL, FAIRFORD:
   July 11. 1883.

CONTENTS

OF

THE FIRST VOLUME.

CHAPTER		PAGE
I.	EN ROUTE FOR THE CAUCASUS	1
II.	THE BLACK SEA AND KUTAIS	44
III.	THROUGH RADCHA	72
IV.	KEERTEESHO	118
V.	SHUKACHÂLO	154
VI.	BY THE SOURCE OF THE RION	195
VII.	LAPÛR TO USHKÛL	237

ILLUSTRATIONS TO VOL. I.

VALLEY OF THE RION   *Frontispiece*

VILLAGE OF CZIRMICHI .   *To face page* 76

PERSIAN GIPSY MUSICIANS   ..   162

BRIDGE OF KIDESKALE   230

CHAPTER I.

EN ROUTE FOR THE CAUCASUS.

'*Okhota khooje nevolia!*' (the chase is worse than slavery) was the refrain running through the last pages of my first book on sport in the Caucasus. And, indeed, when those words were dinned into my ears, at the fag end of the wet season on the Black Sea coast, by a gillie who was sulky and homesick, in the service of a master pulled down by hardship and diphtheria, I was heartily ready to acknowledge the truth of the proverb. But to the sportsman, as to the slave, freedom from his bonds can bring no lasting happiness. The freed slave is, if history and travellers lie not, a slave into whom have entered seven devils worse than the first. Freedom to him means aimless idleness, and idleness misery. So too with the hunter of big game. However much he may have felt the hardships which wait on the worship of the woodland goddess, he has but to shake her fetters off to find how tame and insipid life would be without them. The limbs which manly toil almost beyond their power had strung and hardened until they were tough as tempered steel, soften when the strain upon them ceases, and fill with aches and pains which they had never known on rugged hillside or forest couch. The bright self-reliant spirits, born of a good digestion, nursed on keen mountain air, spurred into action by difficulties to overcome, rendered buoyant by hard-earned successes, flag and sicken under the influence of ease, idleness, and English feeding, which latter means about twice as many meals per diem as any healthy human being requires.

Beautiful as the forest deity is when you are basking in her smiles, with game in sight on the hillside, or at your feet, as you lie tired but happy in the glow of your blazing pine logs, she seems never so fair, never so irresistible, as when you dream of her, on a day in June, your nostrils choked, and your eyes blinded by the dust that is to be found east of Temple Bar; your ears deafened by the rattle of the traffic, your senses dazed by the passing and repassing thousands, and your fist clenched in a scarcely controlled desire to knock down any of the hundred and one black-coated annoyances, who incessantly blunder up against you or poke their umbrellas into your eyes in their mad race against time.

Any summer day in the hateful thoroughfares of our great city would beget in me longings almost beyond control for the free hunter's life, away from towns and the noise of men ; but a summer's day in the city in the year of grace 1882 had a peculiar spur of its own to drive a wanderer out again into the wilds. At every street corner you caught a glimpse of men whose peculiar luggage and radiant faces said, in the plainest language of their own plain native tongue. ' Active service, thank God ; we're in for some fun at last.' Every paper was full of the news of war, every tongue busy talking of it, every shop full of the bustle of it, so that unless a civilian against his will wanted to die of *ennui* and scarlet fever, there was nothing for him but to bury himself, out of reach of the stirring sounds, in the restful quiet of the forest and the silence of the mountain side.

The year before, a neatly worded advertisement had tempted me to join an expedition towards the North Pole in company with about a score of other trustful Englishmen and women. We were to stay seventeen days at Spitzbergen, and slay white bears and walrus and reindeer. Those for whom a forty-pound salmon could not afford sufficient excitement were to help man the whale-boat, and assist in the capture of the leviathan himself. But the expedition had resulted in failure; the seventeen days had been curtailed to three, and my own visions of ice-bears and reindeer had ended almost as disastrously as the dreams of the Isaac Walton of our party, who had come armed with a vast supply of mighty salmon rods, and furnished with great stores of wondrously coloured flies (made after a pattern supplied by the arch humbug who got up the expedition), with which to angle in a land wherein not only did we find no fish but no rivers to hold any.

One experiment of this kind is enough for a lifetime; so that the advertisements of gentlemen about to conduct others to distant lands for the sake of sport, having no longer any attraction for me, it hardly needed the advice of a too flattering reviewer to prove to me that duty and pleasure alike demanded that I should revisit my old hunting grounds in the Caucasus, and endeavour to extend my acquaintance with that neglected country.

I had now tried hunting gregariously, and found that pleasant in theory but unprofitable in practice; I had tried the life of a solitary hunter, and found solitude irksome at times, but always conducive to good sport; now it was decreed that I should try a middle course. A parliament of ladies decided for me that my 'valuable' life was not to be entirely trusted to my own keeping, and if I ever hoped for leave of absence from home, I must first find myself a stalwart friend and companion, to cheer me in my privations and insert his burly person between me and all possible danger. Brother sportsmen! if I confide to you that the premier of that parliament of dames was my much-dreaded wife, you will not wonder that I submitted at once to its decree, and in the shortest possible time produced my friend—a sturdy, cheery-looking sportsman from a neighbouring hunt—whose ruddy countenance seemed to repudiate the possibility of low spirits, and whose digestion has been described by one who had been sharing with him the early rising pleasures of 'cubbing' in September as never so fit as when it commenced its day's work with a couple of large green apples and a short black pipe, between five and six in the morning. Alas that there ever should be a place where even green apples and black pipes cannot be found to solace the early rising sportsman! But no coming events cast their evil shadows before on the evening of August 2, when full of good spirits, having finished the last miseries of preparation, Frank and I raced in rival hansoms to Victoria. We felt afterwards, when we reached Poti, that possibly profession has more influence than race on the character of individuals, for drunk as our British cabbies were in London, those who piloted our droschky at Poti were more drunken still.

Having tried all other routes to Russia and found them fairly quick and comfortable, I elected this time to try the Flushing route; but though we had a fair passage on the crowded boat, not even immunity from the attacks of my most dreaded enemy, *mal de mer*, will induce me to prefer the Flushing route to that by Paris. Still it was a change to rattle through the watery flats of the Netherlands (glorious haunts for the wild fowler, I should fancy, in the winter), our train seeming to be the only thing that was in a hurry in steady-going Holland, where the whole country side looks like one huge home farm, so trim and neat is it, with its long straight avenues of poplars, its very plough horses in fly-cloths, neat and trim as a parlour-maid's apron, and everything in art and nature suggestive of restful prosperity. It was a change too for me, and not a pleasant one, to carry with me across the Channel those leaden skies which many years of wanderings had taught me to regard as the special attribute of an English landscape.

Wherever we went my companion twitted me with the cloudy skies so different from those I had prophesied at starting. All the rivers were turbid; even the Rhine was red with mud, and the whole country rain-drowned. The view from a railway window blurred with rain is not a cheery one, so it is small wonder that Frank and I hibernated for those four days between London and Odessa, and the memory of them to me at least is like that of any other restless sleep, except for the perpetual recurrence of that ghostly face at the window, requiring every quarter of an hour or so to see our tickets.

The only place at which we were compelled to make any long stay *en route* was Oswiecin, on the Austrian frontier—a delay neither of us regretted—for Oswiecin is a quaint old place, with one or two things worth seeing in it, and our legs wanted stretching badly. At first sight Oswiecin appeared to be entirely populated by Jews and the beast the Jew professes to abhor. Every part of the town near the station on the day of our arrival was thronged with droves of swine, so many and of such various breeds as you would seldom find together elsewhere. The pig of the place, too, was unique—a tall, white beast, with a long curling coat, which I should imagine would almost pay for shearing.

In the town the entire population appeared to be Jewish. Indeed, as we neared Russia, and in Russia itself, all along the line up to Odessa the stations were thronged with Jews, creatures in long, loose dressing-gowns, with an oily curl behind each ear, reaching to the shoulder, like the ringlets worn by women fifty years ago, and on their heads a wide-awake of greasy black velvet.

I have no wish to revive the discussions on the merits of the Jew persecutions in Russia, but, as coming fresh from the society of Russians and some of the towns in which those persecutions took place, I can hardly refrain from saying that I should think the authors of the accounts which appeared in the papers must have been themselves Jewish, so one-sided and exaggerated do they appear to have been. Whatever was the true history of this outbreak of anti-Semitic feeling, I am afraid that only a very small portion of the hatred of the Russian for the Jew has as yet found vent and exhausted itself. We ought in justice to Russia to remember that she has far more than her share of the Jewish race, and however admirable their unity as a race, in spite of their want of a fatherland, through so many centuries may appear to us, to those amongst whom the Jews live it may seem that the children of Israel owe their unity to that intense selfishness which puts them always, indirectly at any rate, in antagonism with those races amongst whom and upon whom they are living.

Russia wants soldiers and agriculturists. The Jews are neither one nor the other. That they were a warlike people once, history assures us and we believe; but the least acquaintance with the Jew of to-day will show that he is the least warlike of men. As agriculturists they are even worse. Take the Talmudical Jews of the Crimea, for example. These men are descendants of Jews deported from the Polish provinces by the Russian Government, 'in order' (I quote here from Rev. J. Milner's 'Crimea') 'to weed them (*i.e.* the Polish provinces) from a race of unscrupulous dealers, and reclaim the migrants to honest industry by agricultural employment.

'Holding every class of manual labour in abomination, and never taking to field work wherever there is a chance of driving a trade, the children of Abraham have gradually slunk off from the rural localities and crept into the towns, hanging themselves on to the better class of inhabitants, until a subsistence can be gained by traffic in all sorts of trifles.'

Naturally, then, Russia and Russians do

not love those who are useless to them, who live on them as parasites, and yet, though parasites, despise and hold aloof from those they prey on.

But let me leave the Jew. He is too serious a subject for my pen, and I own, in all honesty, I am no fair judge of him or his doings, the mere sight of him putting up my hackles almost as much as the sight of a cat puts up those of a fox terrier. I don't know why it is, but I fancy it is because he won't cut his hair, and has a predilection, though of the masculine gender, for wearing ringlets and petticoats.

In Oswiecin there is a fine, broad stream full of trout and salmon, so the natives say, which might perhaps be worth a visit to some of those who cannot now afford a fishing in Scotland or even a river in Norway; and should the angler be by chance an antiquarian also, he will find matter for investigation in the ruins of a massive old Dominican church and a feudal castle of many hundred years ago, which look down from a height on Oswiecin and its river.

The last twelve hours of the journey into Russia, if performed at night, are unique in railway travel. About every hour and a half the train pulls up at a pointsman's hut, situated in a forest or on a steppe, far from any village or town. Here the guard gets down, and, if one may be allowed to judge from appearances, goes to wake up the slumbering pointsman. Having got him up, the pointsman performs his office, and then we move slowly on to wake the next, another thirty miles off—how slowly may be gathered from the fact that for the first verst or so a pack of curs, who seem to depend mainly on the liberality of railway passengers for subsistence, follow the train like gulls in the wake of a ship.

The worst part of a journey of this kind from England to Russia is the difficulty of passing your guns through the Custom House on the Russian frontier—a difficulty which we overcame, thanks to the intervention of my kind friend, Consul-General Stanley at Odessa, and the payment of 7*l.* for our four firearms.

I should strongly recommend future travellers to ship their rifles, and in fact almost all they needed to take with them, direct for Odessa; where, having an English consul on the spot, and not being at all hurried, they would have far less trouble with their goods than if they attempted to bring them with them overland.

Of course, if you are in no hurry, and have not yet seen the beauties of the Bosphorus, a voyage *viâ* Constantinople direct to Batoum is by far the most luxurious way of reaching the Caucasus; and, I believe, considerably cheaper than the overland route.

But then the voyage takes, I think, from a fortnight to three weeks, while by rail a third of that time suffices.

But whatever you do, don't trust to the chance of obtaining any of your sporting appliances in Russia. Even at the best shops guns, rifles, and all other sportsmen's tools are cheap and nasty; and unless you can take your own powder with you from England, you are little likely to get anything fit to shoot with in the Caucasus and Southern Russia.

The steamers from Odessa to Poti only run twice a week during the summer, while in winter they do not even do that as a regular thing. Small storms have a great effect on the minds of Russian mariners; the harbours along the Black Sea coast are none of them very good, so that communication by water between Odessa and Poti is often interrupted.

With true travellers' luck, the train we

had missed at Berlin cost us three days' delay at Odessa. To sit still in our hotel and be patient, now that we were just on the borderland of our happy hunting grounds, was impossible.

Odessa has few charms for the sightseer; Frank hated sightseeing, and I had seen all the sights before, so that there was no hope of dispelling *ennui* by 'doing the lions.' But half an hour's chat with my old friend Consul-General Stanley put us in a more hopeful mood. To do him justice, our consul is a thorough Englishman, always ready for sport when he can be spared from the duties of a busy consulate; so that before the morning was over we were all *en route* for the snipe marshes of the Dnieper, full of the memories of our last visit to them in 1876, and sanguine of sport on the morrow in spite of the prophecies of too much water and no birds, which stay-at-home Odessa sportsmen had dinned into our ears before starting.

A drive of fifty miles or more over wastes of land more arid and more devoid of game than a London brickfield, is wearisome work, though for a new comer, like my friend, a good deal of amusement may be derived from the driver's shifts to make ends meet in the oft repaired, always breaking rope-harness, and some excitement from the knowledge that the off-wheeler is galloping on the pavement, his heels about on a level with the driver's head, while the rest of the team is going freely in the road below. But these are things you get used to in Russia, as you do to the subsequent admission of your driver that he has not the faintest notion of the way, and that there is a good chance of your having to spend the night on the steppe.

'How often, oh, how often!' as the song says, have I got into a droschky in Odessa, and told the Jehu to take me to such and such a street. 'Xarocho' ('All right') is the answer, and off you go up one street and down another, until it suddenly occurs to you that this is by no means the direction in which you had been led to believe your destination lay. On inquiry you will find your driver has not a notion where the place is you want to get to, and has only refrained from admitting his ignorance for fear of losing his fare. So it was on this occasion; and in the gloaming we found ourselves wandering about on the steppe, no landmarks in sight, no village near, and still no sign of that long line of marshland on the horizon wherein Troitsky is situated.

Up to this point there had been little enough in the drive to repay us for the dust and the bone-shaking we had endured. Odessa itself, which took a long time getting out of, is not a thing of beauty, though over and over again

I have heard Russians seriously contend that, next to Paris, it is the finest city in the world. A more mathematically ugly town, with straight streets of cold, cheerless-looking houses, could not by any chance be set on the hideous dusty flat which surrounds it. Outside Odessa the scene is more ugly than that within its walls, for the monotony of colour and intense flatness continues, while life apparently ceases altogether.

This year, owing to the extreme heat, every particle of vegetation had been dried up; there were no quails, owing (the people said) to the failure of the crops; and the only live things between Troitsky and Odessa seemed to us to be a few solemn-looking, red-legged cranes, in half-mourning, stalking about in search of the lively frog, who was not. These birds have a free pass everywhere, and no reckless sportsman or mischievous urchin ventures to molest them. Each of the old pillars of the former gateways of Odessa, opening on to the steppe, bears the cumbrous and untidy burden of their nests; and again and again during the day we came upon small, whitewashed cottages which appeared to have been made the foundation of a considerable woodstack. On the top, in meditative mood, stood the stork, as self-possessed and as much at home as the human bipeds who dwelt beneath his nest. But if we had not had very ample food for conversation, the drive from Odessa to Troitsky would have been insupportably dull. The sport within reach of residents at Odessa, we found from our friend, was by no means to be despised; two hundred and fifty woodcock in a week, to two guns, being sufficient almost in itself to tempt men to visit Odessa. In the neighbouring government of Podolia, too, wolf-shooting drives are organised on a grand scale, to say nothing of a more exciting form of wolf hunt, peculiar, I believe, to the country; in which, having found and roused their wolf on the bare, treeless steppe, the hunters, being well mounted, attempt to ride him down.

As there are no coverts or other places of refuge open to the quarry, and the steppe is all good going for the horses, it is not long before the leading horsemen draw up to the wolf. But the game is far from over yet. Though the hunters might easily spear or shoot the wolf, no one attempts to do either; but as soon as he begins to show signs of distress they slacken their pace, and content themselves with keeping just near enough to him to oblige him to do his best. At last even under these circumstances the brute's heart and wind fail him, and he lies down. Then one of his pursuers, riding up, whips the beaten beast into motion again, and so the chase goes on until, utterly exhausted, no whipping can get another trot out of the wolf.

When this happens, the feat of the day has to be performed, and cool and quick must the man be who achieves it successfully. The object of the hunt is to secure the wolf alive, and for this, when he lies down for the last time, the nearest horseman dismounts, and approaching the wolf from behind pins him behind the ears with his naked hands, and so holds him fast while the rest of the party muzzle and bind him. Then they carry him home all alive, oh! What they do with him when they get him there deponent sayeth not.

Apropos of this kind of sport, there was some years ago at St. Petersburg a Captain H., who used to treat Bruin in a somewhat similar fashion. As the ordinary methods of bear-slaying may have become stale and flat to some of our hot-blooded Nimrods, let me offer them this new recipe. Immediately after the first fall of snow, Captain H., who was a wonderful expert on snow shoes, used to leave his quarters in St. Petersburg and seek the thinly peopled districts of Finland. Here the peasants knew and liked the Petersburg Nimrod well, and soon found for him the tracks of his old enemy in the new snow.

Once on the bear's track, Captain H. asked no more help from any living man, but, armed only with a broad-bladed spear, glided away on his snow shoes, through scattered woods of birches, through silent pine forests, and over dreary steppe lands, taking no trouble about the wind, or silence, or any other of the many conditions to be observed by the ordinary stalker, for his object was not to creep on his prey unawares, but rather, following him in all his devious wanderings, to fairly run him down.

Once roused from his fancied solitude, the bear would do all he knew to escape, but, fast though he is on firm ground, he would have little chance against a man on snow shoes over new fallen snow. At every step he took, the bear's weight would make him sink almost to the shoulder, and, however great his strength and pluck, he would soon be exhausted in such heavy going as this. But Captain H. knew the nature of his game too well to try to run him to bay at first, and contented himself with keeping the bear always moving in front of him, sticking like fate to the weary beast's track, sleeping on it at night and resuming it again at dawn, until on the second or third day, when he viewed his game, the bear was almost too dead beat to crawl.

When at last neither shouts nor the near approach of his enemy could get another trot out of 'old Michael,' when he had been fairly run to a standstill, the time had arrived to use the spear, and, risky as it may appear, Captain H. used to make very light of the dangers he had run during the many seasons he had hunted bears in this fashion. Once only, when his snow shoes, catching in a half-buried log, sent him diving head first into Bruin's lair on the lee side of the log, was he in any real danger, and even then the bear seems to have been as glad to part company with his unwilling visitor as even that visitor could wish.

But to return to our own adventures. The evening had already deepened into night, and our watches, seen by the light of the last fusee, told us it was nearly ten o'clock, when we managed to hit upon the end of that long street of irregular houses which goes by the name of the village of Troitsky. But though we had found Troitsky we seemed as far as ever from finding shelter for the night. All the lights were out, all the villagers in bed, and do what we would, we could not rouse them or recognise the hut in which Odessa sportsmen are always wont to put up. So we drove backwards and forwards up a weary verst of unlit village street, serenaded by a pack of the noisiest curs in Russia.

At last, when all hope of a cheery tea and comfortable bed had vanished for the night, a door opened and a peasant looked out to see what the noise was about. We caught at the chance as a drowning man catches at a straw, but all our blandishments were in vain. Nothing would induce the stolid brute to turn out and show us the way. The dogs would tear him to pieces on his way home, he said, and, though no doubt he exaggerated, the stoutest stick is insufficient protection against these famished brutes at night; and when we at last secured a guide, he brought his horse with him, though the distance to be travelled was but a few hundred yards, in order that he might have his legs at a safe distance from his barking followers when he returned.

It was no wonder that we could not find Theodore's house, for since our last visit it had been burnt down, and Theodore himself was lodging next door with his brother, in whose house we found as cleanly a room and as cheery a welcome as any peasant's house in Southern Russia ever affords. Late as it was, that one comfort of the Russian's life, the samovar, was soon aglow, and, soothed by the fragrant odours of tea and cigarettes, even Frank did not seem to consider our first night in Russia likely to put too severe a strain on our endurance, and was ere long treating us to a lovely nocturnal solo, which lasted without intermission until breakfast time.

Mr. S. had some theory about insects and newspaper which I did not completely understand, but the result of it was that he passed the night on a bed he had brought with him, rolled up bodily in a newspaper, and a livelier or more noisy edition of the 'Times' never was issued than the one in which he tossed and prayed for the whole insect creation through the livelong night.

In the pride of my heart, I had said, as I turned in on the floor about 11 P.M., 'Fleas don't bite me,' but I ate my words before morning, and no one of the three was more delighted than myself when the strong morning sun blazed in through the uncurtained window and turned us all out at 5.30 into the delicious freshness of a morning breeze off the lake, whilst all the world was still in the first glow of its waking good spirits, and the fizz had not yet gone off the newly opened day.

When we rise at home, as a rule birds and beasts have already been up so long that, if they are not half weary, the first exuberance of their waking gladness has at least calmed down, the flowers have lost some of their freshness, and even the morning breeze is less crisp and keen than it was at dawn. Only sportsmen and early farm labourers get the best of the day, and we here in Troitsky, even at 5.30 A.M., were 'last down' in the village. Red-petticoated women with bare feet were already drawing water at the well, or tending the creatures of their home farm, driving the hissing geese to the lake side, or giving chanticleer and his family their morning feed of maize. Grave storks, red-legged and billed, who had come back from their breakfast on the steppe some half an hour ago, looked a reproachful good morning at us from their woodstack on the housetop, and our guides for the day were both down by the waterside hard at work mending their nets an hour before their lazy employers appeared on the scene.

The evil reports which we had heard in Odessa were unfortunately not without foundation. All the best of the snipe-ground was under water, so that we had to launch a crazy old boat and go cruising about in the marsh, seeking a dry place to land upon. Far as the eye could see, to right and left of us, stretched the great marsh, gleaming water and tall reed forests dividing the space pretty equally between them, the sky above alive with flights of fowl, whose wild cries made sweet music to the sportsman's ear, while on the far other side, from a blue morning mist, the neat villages of the Bessarabian hills peeped out. A punt gunner might have filled his boat from the stands of peewit and flocks of sandpipers on the mud flats which we passed on our way, but our minds were intent on snipe; and unless one of these came rocketing overhead, or a curlew for once forgot his ordinary caution, our guns were allowed to lie idle until we reached our destination. Then the fun was fast and furious. The moment your foot was on shore the birds rose in whisps, and so bewildered me personally that I shot like a tinker for almost the whole of the morning. Not only were all the birds on the wing at once, but the places in which we found them were so small that long before we had time to steady down they had all gone, so that twice I went back to the boat emptyhanded and disgusted. Frank shot fairly well, but, except with him, I think in the morning the snipe had decidedly the best of it.

In spite of the water, these marshes are full of people. Not only do you hear continually the report of the native fowler's piece, and see at every turn men sitting patiently angling or trimming the clever reed nets with which the water is full, but every reed jungle has its system of water ways, along which you meet the people of the marsh trudging as contentedly knee-deep from village to village as if they were on dry land. In one deep thoroughfare in which I was going daintily, trying at least to keep my knickerbockers dry,

I met an old grey-beard, lame of one leg, with his clothes and a pack on his back, wading happily along, followed by two of the women folk of his family; and from time to time throughout the day we came across parties of village men and maidens, the latter exceedingly tall and shapely, bare limbed, and with petticoats held if anything higher than a ballet-dancer's, and as little ashamed of themselves as Eve in Eden. The example was infectious, and ere long I too was taking my wetting as nature meant me to, keeping a reserve of dry clothes to fall back upon in the cool of the evening; and though the others stuck to their garments, they plunged just as recklessly as I did into holes waist-deep in their anxiety to get to a likely spot.

Our best sport during the day was in a strip of willow plantation, where, though the shooting was of the hardest, it was as pretty as any I have ever seen. Birds were extremely plentiful, and seldom went right away; but unless you were quick enough to kill them almost as soon as flushed, they slipped behind a tree, and your only other chance was a long shot as they cleared the tops of the willows. Here we all came to time and shot much better; and had we only found this little paradise earlier in the day, our bag would have been far heavier.

During the day we saw very few ducks, and except for an otter which Frank chased persistently for a quarter of an hour over the mud flats and through the reed forests, no sign of any four-footed game, although I am convinced these reeds shelter more game than they are usually credited with—one comparatively small reed bed near Kertch containing at least one pack of wolves, an abundance of foxes, and until a friend of mine killed him, a remarkably fine lynx. In the Caucasus these reed beds are favourite haunts of wild swine and red deer, but by daylight you can do nothing with the game, and any attempt to lie in wait for them at night would be rendered futile by clouds of the hungriest mosquitoes in Asia.

Of all the denizens of the marsh the bull-frogs were the noisiest, and a tyro might be forgiven some momentary misgivings if he felt them, when a sudden chorus of these creatures, till then unheard and unsuspected, bellowed forth their displeasure as he unwittingly intruded on their domains. Like all other Russian sporting guides, ours had brought their guns, and though their weapons were the most primitive muzzle-loaders, though they measured shot and powder by hand alone, and plucked the damp grass of the fen for wads, I don't think the snipe had a much better chance with them than with our breech-loaders.

On our way back several big oily rises

just at the edge of the reeds made me long to change the gun for the rod for one short half hour; and as I could not do this I contented myself with carrying home another angler's spoil—a splendid fish, of the carp species, about five or six pounds in weight, which I purchased for about sixpence, to be converted two hours later into an excellent soup by our hostess. I never knew carp were worth eating before, but in my humble opinion, though no great judge in matters concerning the table, all Russians possess a special talent for cooking fish. When we reached the lake-side, and spread out our spoils, we found we had fifty-five snipe and eleven various, including two double snipe—a bag extremely small for a place in which it is on record that a single gun killed his one hundred couple in a day, thus eclipsing Prince S——'s seventy-five couple at Sebastopol; but a bag with which any reasonable sportsman might well be as content as we were.

Snipe-shooting, like other things, has two sides to it, and though plunging about barelegged in the more than tepid water was pleasant enough all day, I had to suffer bitterly for it all night. Of course, those garments which I had taken such care to preserve from a wetting had got sodden by the partial filling of our leaky old boat, so that having no change of clothes, I was obliged to sup in a costume the lower portion of which had been supplied by our good-natured hostess; the male portion of the village never appearing to possess a duplicate pair of the most necessary articles of clothing. The fun at my expense in my loose pink and white attire was naturally unbounded; but this was harmless compared to the agony I endured from my inflamed legs. Without my feeling it at the time, the sharp-edged reeds had not only grazed all the skin off my shins, but covered them with a number of fine deep gashes, into which the water (by no means pure) had soaked; and this, together with the blistering effect of a hot sun on my wet skin, had set up an inflammation which did not entirely subside for weeks, and nearly drove me mad at the time. Of course, when it was too late, my guide, who had watched me wading all day, told me that even the natives of the marsh suffer if they wade bare-legged in it for more than an hour or so at a time, and from my own experience I can well believe him.

Before leaving Troitsky next morning, I had a stroll round the village, and found it, like most of its fellows of this fen-land, composed of two or three long rambling streets, built on the high land, at right angles to the marsh and immediately overlooking it. The houses are all reed-thatched. If they have a yard attached, the yard is fenced in with a neat barrier of woven reeds; reeds form the mats that cover the floor; reeds make the baskets and many of the household utensils of the family; the good man of the house catches the fish that form the staple of the village food, in funnel-shaped traps made of the very reeds wherein his victim had formerly his holt; and altogether the reeds become a feature not only in the landscape which surrounds them, but in the very life of the peasants.

The houses themselves, without exception, are of one storey, having the floor divided into two rooms—a living room which comprises bed, dining, and sitting room all in one, and a kitchen. The outside of the houses alone admits of variation, and here the householder gives his fancy full play, and paints his abode in all the colours obtainable at the shop of the colourman of Odessa. Most of the villagers in these Dnieper villages seemed to have a small vineyard attached to their cottages, and all had their garden and their corn-patch allotted to them on the adjoining steppe. Men and women alike are at work all day, the men fishing on the lake or working in the fields, the women mending nets, tending the cattle, or busy on the threshing floor; and I never remember to have seen a more prosperous village than Troitsky. So far as I could see, there was only one liquor-shop in it, and not a single Jew, while every one seemed as healthy and happy as simple folk who work hard in a bracing atmosphere ought to be. I even met an old Russian here, who refused my offer of a cigarette, and spoke scornfully of the use of the pleasant weed as a modern habit and a filthy one, fit only for idle boys; he himself, he said, remembered the time when no good true-believing Russian moujik ever knew how to smoke. Times are indeed changed since then, if this venerable anti-tobacconist spoke truth, for to those who know him, the Russian peasant's character would seem incomplete without that smoke in which more than half his time is wasted, half his energy dissolved. As our horses were being harnessed I tried to elicit a little local information from my old friend, who was hard at work on the other side of the fence driving a team of unshod horses round and round over the hardened mud of his threshing-floor, to separate the golden grain from the chaff. The horses he was driving were young ones, three of a drove of ten, which were the pride of the old man's heart. They were like the rest of the horses owned by the peasants in this part of Russia (and here I quote a better judge of horseflesh than myself), rather well-bred looking screws, under fourteen hands, and very faulty about the shoulders; but a little experience soon proves that they are better than they look;

and a poor brute, who has been driven as all horses are here, since he was two years old, and fed on nothing but hay, for the most part, will do a better day's work than an ordinary corn-fed English trapper.

Forty-five roubles (two pounds ten shillings) was about the average price of the horses at Troitsky, when we were there, but then horses were selling at lower prices than usual, owing to the scarcity of fodder. For the same reason a cow with her calf by her side could be bought for the same price. Altogether, though he told me he could clear as a rule about 300 roubles a year on his eight desiatine (2·86 acres) of land, my patriarchal friend did not seem much more contented with farming prospects than his brother agriculturists in England.

CHAPTER II.

THE BLACK SEA AND KUTAIS.

There is an old friend of mine out in the East for whom I think I ought to say a word, if by chance any word of mine can do aught to restore to her the character of which she has been most unjustly robbed. No one loves less than I do 'the deep and dark blue ocean.' Its freshening breezes are to my mind inseparable from a memory of the smell of the engine room; its boundless plain only suggestive of the confined daily walk on deck. But if ever there was one section of the briny element less objectionable than another, it is the much maligned Black Sea. Often and often have I trusted myself on its bosom, though never except under compulsion and with a distinct feeling of dread. But though I have known it all the year round, it has never played me false yet, nor robbed me of my daily bread to feed its scaly hordes.

When Frank and I got back to Odessa our steamer lay at the pier, and far as the eye could see, the waves had assumed a glassy, immovable appearance, inexpressibly comforting to the heart of the timid mariner; so that with light hearts we hurried through what business we had to perform, and with a letter of introduction to the most influential sportsman in the Caucasus safe in our keeping, turned our backs on Odessa full of the most sanguine hope for the future. A cruise round the coast of the Crimea and Caucasus in brilliant summer weather, on a comfortable, well found Black Sea steamer, is a distinctly pleasant experience, and we enjoyed it to the full. At

Sebastopol we landed for a few hours, and heard great accounts of its increasing importance as a trading port, the consular fees for the year being double those of preceding years.

At Yalta much of the old bustle and life seemed extinct. Most of its popularity and prosperity passed away with the life of the late Emperor, and the big hotels were more than half empty and the gaily attired Tartar horse-boys, beloved of Russian ladies, lounged about in picturesque idleness, there being none to hire them or their ambling steeds. Yalta, too, had suffered from the destruction of Orianda, the Grand Duke Constantine's country seat, the blackened skeleton of which we caught a glimpse of in passing, half hidden amongst its groves of beautiful trees.

Kertch was as picturesque and more prosperous than ever, while Novo Rossisk, four years ago a lifeless, unimportant village, has now, thanks to the American Petroleum Company at Taman, grown into a bustling, prosperous town. At Kertch we heard the wail of a parched country over the summer now passing away. Ten days before our advent the thermometer there had shown 120° Fahrenheit in the shade, and at Theodosia water had been sold in the streets at so much the glassful. All vegetation was burnt completely off the hillsides, and no one in Kertch had heard of such a summer for forty years. The Caucasus was represented as having been, and still being, a little hotter than Hades, so that our heads ached at the mere thought of what was before us ere we could gain the cool neighbourhood of the snow peaks.

The mouth of the Rion at Poti is never very beautiful, with its banks of black mud showing above its dark and sluggish waters; its thickets of thorn and scrub growing densely on either hand, suggestive in their rank luxuriance of nothing but fever and wild swine; but the mouth of the Rion at 4 A.M., the hour at which the Black Sea Steam Company, with its usual perversity, insisted on landing us, was, if anything, less attractive than ever.

The last words of my kind friend, Dr. Schauer, of Kertch, were still ringing in my ears when I landed: 'Above all things don't miss your train at Poti,' so that I was more than ordinarily speedy in piling my small luggage and my friend in a heap in the one droschky which the town had produced for the benefit of the steamer passengers, and after five minutes spent in securing my heavier luggage from the clutches of the crowd of hungry-looking lightermen who swarmed on the quay, I hurried off to the English Consulate. Here, though of course no one was up at that time in the morning, I was admitted, and came upon a scene calculated to dash the spirits of any traveller. On a bed, scarcely strong enough to make himself heard in a whisper, was my old friend the Vice-Consul of Batoum, knocked all to pieces by fever, throwing up blood in quantities, and apparently already at his last gasp. I never expected to see him again, and it was with a heavy heart and no very pleasant bodings for my own future that I hurried away to make sure of the first train which could convey me and mine from the most uninviting looking spot on God's earth. I am happy to be able to say here that my friend did recover, and when we next met at Batoum was almost himself again.

On our way to Kutais we had the luck to interest a Russian fellow-traveller in ourselves and the object of our journey; and he there and then offered us introductions to people who could assist us to obtain sport, and invited us to stay with him for a fortnight's shooting on our way home, on the shores of the Black Sea. This was the second invitation of the kind which we had received since we left Odessa, and I am bound to say that the traveller and sportsman is more likely to be hindered by the very number of kind friends he will meet with in the Caucasus, than to be baffled for want of a helping hand.

I'm afraid I can't say a good word for the officials of the Poti Tiflis railway. They seem to me to be a dreamy, muddle-headed lot. On this occasion their particular iniquity was the sending of my luggage right through to Tiflis at their own expense and to my great discomfort, although I had taken every care to have it sent to Kutais, and was in possession of their ticket, on receipt of which they were bound to deliver my goods to me at Kutais.

If I might venture to make a suggestion to such great ones as the directors of a railway, it would be that they should forbid the use of cigarettes by their clerks in office hours. In this way, though clerks would be almost impossible to obtain, they would not, when obtained, keep the passengers waiting ten minutes at their office windows for their tickets, whilst preparing their tobacco, and might issue one ticket in ten without any gross mistake.

After depositing my friend and what luggage we had with us at the hotel, I availed myself of the offer of a gentleman whose acquaintance I had made within the last thirty seconds, and drove with him up to the station telegraph office to beg the authorities at Tiflis to send back my errant trunks with what speed they could. As the station telegraph office is a place in which a clerk is likely to be wanted on the arrival of a train, it hardly surprised me to find no clerk in attendance. For about twenty minutes my friend and I waited; he passing the time in loud denunciations of the general mismanagement of all business in Russia, while I got through several cigarettes in sulky silence.

At last the clerk came. A tall, dark lady of a somewhat masculine type, but still distinctly a beauty, if she had not, in her passion for woman's rights, cut her hair to the unbecoming length of a schoolboy's, who has evaded the monthly barber. She gave us a gracious bow, made a trifling apology for her absence as she nibbled at a fine bunch of grapes which she was carrying; and then, having arranged what was left of her back hair, and fixed the blind so that the light was exactly to her liking, she sank gracefully into her chair before the telegraph instrument, and proceeded, smiling sweetly all the while with her admirable dark eyes, to catechise me as to the whence, whither, and wherefore of my journey. Now I hope I am as devout an admirer of the fair sex as any of my countrymen, but I appeal to my readers, is this the way to receive a bustling anxious Englishman, who has lost his portmanteau? I think not. At last I got my telegram sent off, and then in sheer gratitude, submitted quietly to a long harangue on the illiberal nature of the British mind, which refuses to admit women to a variety of employments for any and all of which they are better fitted than men. As if to try me to the uttermost she finished by quoting the success of the experiment of the admission of women clerks to employment as telegraphists in Russia and elsewhere. When I left her, if I did not feel sure that women were fit for any office, my doubts were not owing to their fatal want of assurance.

On returning to my hotel, after telegraphing for my stray luggage, I received news of the first of the many strokes of bad luck with which I was to meet in my pursuit of mountain sheep. The Prince of Mingrelia, so his agent informed us, had arranged his great mountain drive for the very week of our arrival; the guests were invited and the cartridges even loaded. And, moreover, thanks to the Prince's well-known courtesy to strangers, not less than to a letter from an intimate friend of his, our invitations to be of the party and a hearty welcome were not matters of doubt.

As I had heard from time to time, like all other travellers in the Caucasus, of these grand battues, at which, so report says, as many as sixty head of tûr (*Capra Caucasica*) and chamois have been killed in a day, I was naturally delighted at the prospect before me, though as an ordinary thing I would consider mountain game far too noble to kill like 'dumb driven cattle,' with no better chance of escaping the bullet than has the running deer at Wimbledon. But my informant dashed my hopes to the ground in the same sentence that gave them birth. At the eleventh hour the Dowager Princess had been seized by a violent illness—so violent, indeed, that all hope of her recovery was abandoned, and of course the drive fell through.

Here, then, was an end to my business at Kutais, ended almost before it was begun. If the Prince's house was to be one of mourning, it was no time for me to hope for assistance in my sporting projects in that quarter. However, being at Kutais I resolved to make that town my basis of operations, and start thence on the morrow for a shooting and exploring trip to Svânetia, that land of mystery and tradition to which comparatively few, even of the Russians, have penetrated; from which those who have been there bring back the wildest stories of a barbarism almost incredible so near the confines of civilisation, and of which one of the reviewers of my last book on the Caucasus, who seemed to know what he was writing about thoroughly, spoke, as a land in which travel would be somewhat dangerous, as well as interesting. In the meanwhile it was nearly time for early risers to turn in, so Frank and I made our way upstairs amidst a chorus of 'good-nights' from our host of newly-acquired friends. But the hospitable inhabitants of Kutais had not done with us yet. In our rooms we found a messenger with a card from the Princess A——, and a message to the effect that the Princess was anxious to make our acquaintance, and would esteem it kind of us if we would come and sup with her. The messenger would conduct us to her house. Now though the hour was more suggestive of bedtime than a first call, cards from princesses had never been so common with Frank and myself as to warrant us in declining the invitation; and though we jostled each other at the little mirror in our room only to come to the conclusion that our appearance savoured more of the railway carriage than was becoming for the occasion, we were obliged, *faute de mieux*, to be content with ourselves, and took ourselves off at once to the august presence.

After five minutes spent in vainly endeavouring to cross the best street in Kutais without getting over our ankles in mud, we found ourselves in the presence of our hostess, a charming lady devoted, as she herself assured us, to horses and Englishmen, in that order. We soon found that we owed our reception to the tongue we spoke, which the Princess had overheard whilst riding past our hotel that evening. After two or three hours spent in pleasant chat we acceded to her suggestion that we should dine with her on the morrow, and then join the shooting party of her nephew, Prince A——, which was to leave Kutais for a drive some thirty versts from the town on the following evening.

Thus our intention of starting for Svânetia was for the first time postponed.

At three punctually on the next day, Frank and I presented ourselves in the last clean collars our journey had left us, little knowing what was in store for us. It seemed, from what the Princess subsequently told us, that there had been a mutiny in the kitchen, and all the servants were at the moment 'on strike.' However, after a considerable amount of diplomacy had been employed by the Princess and her friends (for like a feudal chieftain she seemed to live surrounded by a crowd of relations and retainers), the cook was prevailed on to send in the repast.

The dinner was, I believe, Georgian in style, but was sufficiently like a Russian dinner to need no description here. The drinking, not the eating, is the salient feature in a Caucasian feast. A toast-giver (toolambatch) having been appointed, we took our places at table, eighteen guests in all, and every guest, except an English young lady, the governess of the family, and ourselves, of princely rank.

Having swallowed our modicum of neat spirit which, with some trifling relish, such as a large white radish or piece of salt cheese, forms the necessary prelude of every dinner, we were allowed about five minutes for honest, straightforward feeding. Then the toolam batch arose, and our glasses (small tumblers) having been filled with the red wine of Kakhetia, the toast-giver proposed the health of the Princess. At this all rose, bowed, and clinked glasses with our hostess, emptied the tumblers, struck them loudly on the table; and then the nimble-fingered amongst the men sent their glasses whirling head over heels in the air, to show they were innocent of heel taps, caught them as they descended in their left hands, and replaced them on the

table with a force that made the plates rattle.
Then all sang in chorus a kind of thanksgiving to the giver of the feast, to a tune which sounded rather like a Gregorian chant. In about another minute the glasses were recharged, some one else's health proposed, and the same ceremony performed in its honour. This kind of thing continued until every one's health had been drunk, by which time seventeen honest tumblers had been emptied by each member of the dinner party, no small feat for men not used to large libations.

There was only one trifling distraction during this first part of dinner, which was owing to the bodily peril of a member of the party. One of the princes, it seems, had left the table unobserved, and sought solitude in the yard below the dining-room, whether to escape his fair share of wine or devote his time to hatching an extempore joke still remains a mystery. However, we were roused to a sense of his absence by piercing screams; and on a party being detailed to inquire into the cause, we found the unhappy absentee had been 'baled up' in his bedroom by an irate turkey-cock who, resenting his intrusion in the yard, had violently assaulted and expelled him.

Having released the prisoner, and finding that no one remained to whose health tumblers had not been emptied, the toolambatch rose to the occasion, and showed himself worthy of the public confidence reposed in him. Toast followed toast in rapid succession, until sobriety trembled on its last legs, and instant flight or an ignominious descent below the salt seemed imminent. 'To the health of Madame W.,' said the toolambatch. Clink, clink went the glasses, up they flew, and again the rattling plates recorded another glassful to be atoned for with headaches and soda-water the day after.

'Has Mr. F. got a wife?' whispers the Princess in my ear. 'No,' I return thankfully. The reply is telegraphed to the other end of the table, and the toolambatch, rising gravely in his place, proposes the health of the future Mrs. F., which is hailed with immense applause. Mr. W.'s family, Mr. F.'s future family, our united grandmothers and aunts, and a host of other toasts follow with amazing rapidity, and then to our intense relief the Princess gives the signal, 'cease firing.' 'Just one last glass before we part,' she suggests, and fills for each of us a large port wine glass full of strong liqueur, having done justice to which, with a courage born of despair, Frank and I make our adieux as best we can, and next minute find ourselves congratulating each other on our happy release, and the extraordinarily unnatural phenomenon that we are still able to walk straight.

I forgot in the rattle of the banquet to

mention that about the middle of dinner Prince A—— dropped in to say that owing to some unforeseen circumstance the proposed venue of the hunt would be changed to a forest nearer home, for which reason it would not be necessary to start before early morning on the next day. This was postponement number two.

We thought we had escaped our friends when we reached the shelter of our hotel, but little did we know when we ventured to indulge in such illusive dreams the hospitality of the Caucasian heart, or its rooted aversion to sobriety in a guest. I state a mere fact when I say that not to make a man drunk when he is your guest is looked upon in the Caucasus as a breach of hospitality—a distinct failure in that cordial entertainment for which the country is famed. A Georgian of Radcha, whom I knew well, once said to me in talking of the matter, 'What are we to do? we have no games except cards, no entertainments of any kind; when a man comes to us, we want to make him merry, and nothing does that so well as wine. The process of getting drunk is the pleasantest thing in life, and when he is too far gone to drink any more, we just let him sleep until he is ready to begin again.' This being the spirit of the country, it was small wonder that at the hotel doors we met our host of the morrow's hunt with two other jovial princes, and an array of champagne bottles awful to behold. To refuse was to offend our friends, ruin our reputations as hard-headed Englishmen, and get no shooting at Kutais or help beyond. So with a sigh we submitted to the inevitable, and sat down.

A more perfect linguist than Prince A—— I never met, and his knowledge of English sporting terms was as wonderful as his capacity for champagne. But at last it was over, and the last assault of the enemy having failed to carry the Englishmen off their legs, the princes beat an orderly retreat, and the besieged were allowed to retire with all the honours of war, *i.e.*, the waiter lighted them up to their rooms still sober enough to get their boots off.

So ended the night; but the dawn had hardly commenced when the sound of wheels in the street below and trampling of feet by our bedsides roused us unceremoniously from our slumbers. There they were again, like nightmares before our sleepy vision, the Prince and his companions, looking as fresh as paint, in full sporting costume, with rifles in hand—men, carriages, and dogs all below in the street—begging us to tumble as speedily as possible into our clothes and come down to the street, where their people were waiting to drive us to covert. Already, they urged, we were almost too late. The dawn would be visible in the sky in a few more minutes, the wolves would be back in covert from their midnight maraudings, and if our places were not taken before that, not a wolf would be found to reward our vigil when the beaters came through. So, with scarcely the keenness that the promise of a wolf hunt should rouse in a sportsman's breast, we shook ourselves together, and casting rueful glances at the warm couches from which we had been torn, lit our pipes and prepared for the raw morning air.

At the last moment a head beater came up with a long face to say that the rain had begun to descend in torrents. A long parley here ensued, the result of which was that the hunters voted *nem. con.* a wolf drive in rain only so much labour lost; and assuring us that we should have better luck to-morrow, they all trooped downstairs and rattled off home again in their jolting old droschkies as happy as virtuous princes should be.

For a moment F. and I gazed sadly at one another out of dreamy, unbelieving eyes, and then some one said 'put not your trust in princes;' the other expressing himself to the same effect in more concise and energetic terms, whereafter we retired again to roost, determined that we had seen as much as we cared for of Caucasian toolambatches and princely wolf-hunts.

It is wonderful how the practice of wine-bibbing is interwoven with the whole life of the Caucasus, more perhaps even with its past life than with the life of to-day. Go into any Asiatic shop to purchase ornaments of a bygone time—objects of interest quaintly devised and wrought about with fine silver work—you will find nine out of ten of the things exposed for sale connected with wine drinking in one way or another. All that are not, are weapons or horse trappings; nothing but war, wine, and horsemanship seem to have found favour with the men of old in the Caucasus. On the shopman's walls hang ibex and tûr horns, silver rimmed, and slung in silver chains. These are cups which admit of no heel taps, and were used to test the wind and honest thirst of Caucasian manhood. Beside them hang small gourds encased in open work of black and white silver, their necks so constructed that as the contents flow down the wine-bibber's throat, he is comforted by a gurgling music in the flask. Silver cups and tiny silver goblets for the weaker sex are side by side with these, while on the floor stand huge jars and vases of various shapes in which the red wine was hoarded or brought to table.

If at the present day you ask a Caucasian of the fertility or well-being of any district in his native land, the standard by which he measures its happiness and wealth is its wine-producing capacity. The rich man in the

Caucasus has but little either at Tiflis or Kutais to interest and amuse him, few duties, fewer pleasures. There is no good theatre, the concerts are few, poor, and of a low class; clubs, I think, there are none. He cares little for the chase, and his own stake in his native country has become so small that he cares little for the government of it. The climate is too hot and enervating for any but the most sluggish life to be lived in it, so the rich man solaces himself with wine and tobacco; but wine is his great good.

The peasant's idea of a holiday is a bright day spent basking under the shade of a big walnut tree on a bank outside the village, his friends, male and female, lounging round him; on the grass, an infinite number of little red earthen pots, corked with a bundle of green leaves, to be emptied to the accompaniment of toast and song. A hard head for withstanding the effect of wine is one of the most generally admired physical gifts among these people, and the most popular and influential Englishman who ever lived amongst them was one of whom they will still tell you admiringly that, though he was always thirsty, no toolambatch ever saw him under the table. On one occasion they tell that he and a friend were staying a few days at Piatigorsk, at which fashionable resort a certain beer-loving viceroy arrived two days after the Englishman; but those two days' start had enabled the latter to so drain Piatigorsk of beer that the viceroy had to send to Tiflis for his favourite beverage. This Englishman's brandy cask is still kept by a certain influential Caucasian nobleman amongst his most treasured relics of the past, and many a time with this on his back would its old owner take himself off into the wild mountain fastnesses, and spend days and weeks amongst tribes whose society it would have been unsafe for less privileged persons to court.

There is one thing at least to be said in extenuation of the Caucasian's love of his native wine, which is that it is so pure as to do little or no damage to the drinker, and is not only not a producer of gout in its devotees, but is credited with great healing powers over those afflicted with this disease. I at least can safely say I never met with a gouty man in the Caucasus except such as had come from Russia to cure themselves with 'a hair of the dog that bit them.'

CHAPTER III.

THROUGH RADCHA.

Kutais is not a lively place even for the Caucasus, and seen by eyes that no heavy supper overnight has made captious and hard to please in the morning. To us, then, on the morning after the supper of princes, to us who had endured nearly a week by rail and another by sea, to escape from the trammels of civilised life and revel in wild sport, it seemed so unendurably dull that, in spite of a heavy damp heat reminding one of the interior of a Turkish bath, we set to work with a will to get horses and prepare for a start for Svânetia before dusk.

I was up at six, and by seven had managed to rouse a waiter and send him into the bazaar to make inquiries for horses to take us as far as Oni. By ten a very magnificent Jew, in a shiny peaked cap and diamond studs, came to see us. A glance at him sufficed. He was not the man I wanted, but a rascal who, owning no horses himself, offers to supply them to the unwary at twice the bazaar tariff. If a stranger to Kutais closes with him, he of course sublets his job to a regular horseboy and himself pockets half the money. He very soon found his way down stairs, and unfortunately was so much annoyed at not having been able to do the Englishman, that he went straight off to the assemblage of horseboys, and I believe told them of my imperative need of horses at once, and advised them to put the screw on accordingly. However that may be, it was not till late that I managed to find a man who would undertake to bring me four horses on the morrow, and having stipulated that the horses should be ready at the hotel by six, I reconciled myself to this further delay and ordered dinner, feeling limp and hoarse with the trials of voice and temper to which I had been subjected.

Dinner over, Frank and I set to work to prepare cartridges and pack up what few things we meant to take with us on our journey, which done we turned in ready for an early start on the morrow. But with morning came no horses nor any message from their owner. A protracted search resulted in his appearance about lunch time to say that he had changed his mind, and could not undertake the job for less than double the sum he had agreed for the previous evening. He had heard what the other Jews had been asking us, and was ashamed of the modesty of his own demands. He, too, like the Jew of the diamond studs, was sent out of the hotel a trifle faster than he entered it.

Once more the business of finding a horseboy and making a contract had to be undergone, but with a somewhat better result; for about midday (the fellow having agreed to find four horses and a guide who could speak Russian by 9 A.M.) a Jew, speaking only Georgian, with three (not four) of the sorriest steeds since Rosinante, arrived at our hotel. But we had had enough of bargaining with Jew horsedealers, so we said nothing, but packing ourselves and saddle-bags on the miserable screws, turned our backs on Kutais.

It was a day of insufferable heat, the sun beating down on the low hills round the town in a way that made my head ache in spite of the green leaves inside my helmet and the white towel bound round the outside. The only things with life in them that looked happy were the stolid black buffaloes whose broad backs were just visible above water in some of the shallows of the Rion, and even they were almost too lazy and hot to flap their ears.

For us in our narrow saddles, going at a crawl on animals utterly destitute of any liveliness, always up or down steep inclines, even the beautiful scenery had not much attraction. Sometimes for versts we would wind our way through a succession of straggling villages, half hid in neat well-kept orchards, shut in with wattled fences. The sight of them made our parched lips ache for the fruit which was not yet ripe. The season was not a happy one in some things; too early for fruit and too late to see the dark masses of rhododendron thicket that fringed our path, bright with its yellow blossom. We had been too busy to get anything to eat before starting, so that in spite of the heat, our appetites began

VILLAGE OF CZIRMICH.

to be troublesome long before our day's work was over; but once having made a start we determined to hold out until night compelled a stoppage. Our horses, too, had nothing all day; but to this they seem used, and their owner laughed at the idea of their wanting food before bedtime.

All along our path we met wayfarers either on foot or horseback, many of them in spite of this heat exposing their bare heads to the sun's rays. One fellow, with a dense mass of black hair, trudged bare-headed and barefooted beside us more than half the day, and by taking short cuts and occasionally trotting, oftener waited for our horses than our horses for him. All the men we met gave us a courteous greeting, and here round Kutais all seemed happy and well-to-do.

At last when the sun had long ago set, and the owls were beginning to make themselves heard along our wooded track, we came to a duchân, that is, an open dram shop, a roughly constructed wooden hut, with an open front, in which were displayed half a dozen dirty white bottles partly filled with villainous watki, a bundle or two of dried fish, and a thing like a defunct pig on its back, legs in air, which constitutes the cellar, and is the skin holding all the wine of the establishment. There is another compartment in which a broad board, covered with matting, offers sleeping accommodation to all and sundry, while through a narrow partition they hear their horses busily munching at their hard-earned food. We have seen better inns than this and tasted better wine than the raw red fluid contained in the pig skin, but no rest was ever much sweeter, no wine more refreshing, than that we obtained at the end of our first day's march from Kutais.

C'est le premier pas qui coûte, is peculiarly applicable to the first day's ride in Tartar saddles, and we were heartily glad it was over, and the chickens screaming in the hands of the cook.

Just as the last sounds of the horses' feeding seemed to have ceased, and the half dozen drunken peasants to have become too drunk to shout any more—just, in fact, as our eyes seemed closing, and we were sailing away into regions of dreamless sleep, our Jew roused us with the intelligence that the horses were ready, and if we wanted to get to Oni that day we must start at once.

It was barely dawn, and neither of us were keen to leave our rest so early; but we did it with a grumble—a grumble which on Frank's part was terribly intensified on hearing we were to have no breakfast before starting; none, in fact, until the end of our first stage. This, I think, was the point at which Frank first began to doubt the pleasures of Caucasian travel.

When you are travelling in this country on horseback, and are told that it will take you a certain number of days to reach a particular spot, you must remember that these 'days' are counted from earliest dawn to an hour or so after dusk, and are not ordinary twelve hour days.

We soon found that our resting-place of last night, Tkiboolè, was situated at the foot of a considerable chain of hills, up whose steep sides we had now to climb. So steep were they, and so weak did our ponies appear, that Frank and I at once dismounted, and began the day with a long stiff climb, to which our only objection was that its labours were not shared by our guide who, utterly careless of his horse, sat where he was, smoking placidly. It is to my mind one of the worst traits in the Caucasian character, that these people care nothing for either horse or dog as friends, regarding them as mere machines, only to be noticed with a kick, and never thanked by a caress.

This little climb from Tkibooli to the crest of Nakerala was the only piece of the road between Oni and Kutais over which a droschky might not safely be driven.

At the top of the ridge the road led to a cleft, through which we passed, and as we went we were met full in the face by the delicious free breezes which greet you on every summit, while masses of white mist just tinged with sunlight, came rolling through the pass to meet us. In another minute the whole view burst upon us.

The crest of the ridge is double, and the path winds through a kind of basin between the two ridges, in which grow dense masses of rhododendron thicket, whence rise here and there, tall and gaunt, a few giant pines; one huge white fellow, blasted many a year ago, towering high above the rest. The whole place was wrapt in mist, through which the faint rays of the newly risen sun were diffused, giving a peculiarly wild look to the whole. Along this double crest runs a stream, the Tchaouri, of deep clear water on a bed of silver sand, with an exceedingly sluggish current, in which we were told large quantities of trout were to be found; trout, too, not such as are generally found in mountain burns, but grand fellows of from four to six pounds' weight. But though I looked carefully, and, thanks to considerable practice on the Colne, am by no means slow to mark a rising fish, I never saw a rise, either here or elsewhere, in the three months I was in the country.

Not very far from where the road crosses it, this stream disappears, and after a subterranean course of several versts again emerges. At either end of the subterranean passage the country folk say the trout swarm.

Beyond this stream the forest gradually became more open and the trees larger, many of them being splendid silver beeches of unusual size; others grand pines hoary with age, and festooned with long tresses of silver-grey beard-moss, which, I believe, like ivy and other parasites, kills as it beautifies.

The day we crossed Nakerala happened to be a holiday, and all the folk of the countryside were out enjoying themselves. Hence it happened that as we came down into the lower land we met frequent groups of blue-coated peasants carrying long poles armed with tiny tridents for the spearing of trout. Every male in the villages we passed through seemed to be bent on fishing, and the trout of the neighbouring burns must have had a rough time of it before nightfall. In the villages we found the idle dames of these anglers, clad in many-coloured garments, and hanging about in groups somewhere on the way to the church. Some few here and there drew their face cloths over their faces, but we found this by no means the rule amongst the people of Radcha.

Sigortsminda is one of the prettiest villages on the road—a busy, prosperous-looking place in a well-cultivated plain, with a large lake in its midst. The golden streaks of cultivated land run out on every side, until they meet and are lost in patches of dark forest pine; while far away to right and left roll long stretches of purple hillside, over which in the far distance loom the beautiful snow-peaks of some of the satellites of Elbruz.

The cottages of the village remind you at once of Switzerland, being like them in everything, even to the roofs of plank kept down by boulders. Here we breakfasted; and here I was almost tempted to stay awhile by the accounts of bears in the immediate neighbourhood of Nakerala; and though eventually visions of mountain sheep in the far distant peaks induced me to proceed, I heartily commend Nakerala, with its trout streams and its bears, to any who come after me and don't wish to make too great a toil of their pleasure. From Sigortsminda to Oni was a very weary pilgrimage, our poor little beasts done to a turn, and ourselves tired with much walking, our throats parched with thirst, and our saddles too hot to sit in.

Some of the scenery on the road would amply repay any artist who would visit the country; such views as those of the ruined castles beyond Sigortsminda, and the glimpse of the river Rion as it hurtles along grey and stern between its walls of rugged grey rock at the bridge of Tsess, being hard to beat for beauty in any country. But no one seems to have painted or even photographed the Caucasus, except to such a limited extent as it is seen from the Vladikavkaz road; at least, if they have done so, I have never been lucky enough to come across any of their sketches.

Villages were, luckily for us, of frequent occurrence by the roadside; and in each of these we got a few minutes' rest and a glass of rough wine or water. The heat was at midday almost insufferable, being as much as 160° in the open; and had it not been for these frequent pauses, and the constant recurrence of a kind of plum-tree (*Cornus mascula*), bearing a small round fruit of a brilliant yellow, with the most exquisite flavour imaginable, I don't think we should have reached Oni that day. As it was, Frank was knocked up for a day or two afterwards by his exertions in the sun, and I was almost as bad.

In some of the stony passes on the banks

of the Rion, through which our road lay, were vast numbers of butterflies, almost all of which were new to me. Amongst them were the beautiful swallow tail, a few large copper, and, commonest of all, a very quick-winged vision of loveliness which I have been unable to identify.

Perhaps the prettiest sight which met my eyes all that long summer afternoon was a regular troop of butterflies, swallow tails, and pale clouded yellows, sitting on a small moist patch of ground where a clear little mountain spring fell from the roots of two great ferns into a pool below. The heat was so intense that even these children of the sun had come there, I suppose, for shade and refreshment.

It seemed to me then, and often afterwards, that there is a field open for the entomologist in the Caucasus in which very few have reaped before, and in which a very plentiful harvest is waiting to be gathered in. Herr Radde, the Curator of the Tiflis Museum, has a very good collection of butterflies ; but even I, in my two or three visits to the Caucasus, though but a casual student of entomology, feel convinced that I have seen several varieties in my travels of which there are no specimens at Tiflis.

The daylight was fast departing, though the heat was far from going with it, when my poor little screw stumbled along the last half verst to Oni. Somehow or other my friend and the Jew had fallen behind, but before my mental vision was the hope of a steaming samovar and a refreshing wash ; so, instead of waiting for them, I pushed on alone into the little medley of roughly built wooden houses, called Oni, the capital of the government of Radcha, perhaps the richest in natural productions of any government in the Caucasus.

The governor's house was not much different to the houses round it, but a glimpse of a cool duck uniform on a verandah inclined me to the belief that I had found the house I sought, and a second glance which descried a couple of ladies sitting sipping their tea confirmed my belief. Without more ado I tied up my steed, and, climbing the stairs, saluted the ladies and presented my letter at the duck uniform. Though surprised at first at the extreme directness of my mode of procedure, Baron Geikin—for it was he—became in a moment the most kindly of hosts, putting his house and all that was in it at our disposal at once. But in spite of the tea and rest my voice would not come back for nearly an hour except in dull, hollow tones, which almost frightened their producer. This was, however, the only effect of the long, hot ride, and wore off before morning.

At Oni we spent the night and part of the

next day in engaging horses, and an interpreter, presented to us as a friend by the governor. It was when introducing our interpreter to us that the Baron ventilated a theory, of which we found him very full, that the whole of the tribes of the Caucasus are of Jewish origin, adducing in favour of his theory their personal appearance, the fact that some of the oldest princely families of the Caucasus claim Jewish descent, and that the Jews themselves aver that the Tables of the Law, given to them at Sinai, are now hidden in the Caucasus, three expeditions having been already sent from Amsterdam to seek and recover them. Besides this he alleged that all antique relics found in the Caucasus were Hebrew, and that on every Tcherkess prince's tomb of bygone days you will find the incription, 'Potomka Sudaria Davida'— descendant of the Lord David. Besides this, 'Oori,' which is used in Persian and all Caucasian tongues for Jew, appears constantly in Caucasian names of places, &c., as, for example, 'Gooriel.'

Personally I can vouch for only one of his statements. The inhabitants of the Caucasus are wonderfully Jewish in type, and never more so than when they are beautiful. A beauty of Mingrelia with her raven hair, rather hard black eyes, and aquiline features is as purely Jewish as anything can be in appearance. If they are of Jewish origin, their long sojourn in wild, uncivilised mountain regions has certainly brought out many of the finer traits of the race, which seem to have been lost by the dwellers in towns.

The province of Radcha is, we were told, peculiarly rich in minerals, and efforts are, I believe, being made to attract foreign capitalists to open up mines there. Along our route from Oni, which we left late the following evening, beds of magnificent slate cropped up by the river ; while close by the new bridge spanning the Rion where the road to Glola branches off from the main road to Gebi, we found just on the edge of the grand pine forest fringing the river a spring of strongly impregnated iron water. Near Glola itself is another spring which I did not see, but of which the natives had much to say in favour of its wonderful purgative and other medicinal qualities.

We passed one night, *en route* to Glola, at the little hamlet of Ootsara, although we had to effect a forcible entry at the inhospitable duchân. It was not until the door seemed yielding beneath the sturdy blows of our interpreter, and he seemed every moment likely to be within reach of the innkeeper, whom he was loudly threatening all the while with instant death, that the sleepy old rascal turned out from his lair amongst the pigskins, and let us in.

All the houses in Ootsara are of a temporary character, capable of being transported (*i.e.* what is perishable of them) to warmer climes for the nine months of snow, during which the village is deserted, and indeed buried. Thanks to its mineral springs and delightfully cool temperature, it is rather a favourite resort during the three hot months of the summer; but ruins of rock, patches of shattered forest, and a huge collection of *débris* near the river, told a story of the fury of storm and avalanche to which it is subject in winter.

To say that the scenery on the road to Glola is beautiful would be mere repetition. Wherever you have pine forests, mountains, and a rapid mountain river rushing through all, the scenery must necessarily be beautiful, and these elements of natural beauty you have everywhere along the road from Kutais to Gebi. But for all that the village of Glola may vie with any in the Caucasus for picturesqueness, as the natives say it does for wealth.

In all villages in Radcha and Svânetia there is a house set apart for the use of travellers, which goes by the high-sounding title of 'cancellaria.' High-sounding as the title is, the quarters are generally poor enough—a couple of bare rooms, empty of everything save the live stock left starving on the premises by the last sojourner within their walls, the windows glassless portals to let in the cold night air, and, worse than all, no possibility of privacy. Such is the ordinary cancellaria. That at Glola was no exception to the rule, and in five minutes our kit was deposited on the floor, and our horses tied to the supports of the balcony, whither we had also betaken ourselves, because the room indoors was too dark to be in without a candle, and being little after midday we felt disinclined for artificial light as yet. On the balcony there was light and life enough.

On arriving at Glola we had sent at once for the starchina to whom we had a letter; and as a result of our sending, everyone in the village, except the starchina, was at once in attendance, so that the balcony was as noisy as Babel and as crowded as the Army and Navy Co-operative Stores on Saturday morning.

At Oni everyone had told us that Glola was *par excellence* the home of Bruin; and indeed that they had not altogether lied was evidenced by a couple of fairly fresh skins spread out on a neighbouring cottage; but though there were bears about, we could get no one to guide us to their haunts. Every man in our balcony (and small as it was, it was groaning dangerously under the weight of thirty-one men and a woman) was a hunter; but as they had no dogs to find the bears with, and had had no rain to make the ground sufficiently soft for tracking, and as above all it was for them the only busy part of the year, no one was forthcoming as a guide.

Never having shot bears in any other part of the world I don't know how people manage elsewhere; but for the sake of those who have never seen Bruin at home, I may say here that to go promiscuously into a forest where they are even in large numbers is seldom much good. However quiet you may be, old Michael generally manages to hear you; and big and unwieldy as he looks, a blackbird would make as much noise getting away in the thick bush as he would. Though you almost ran into him, unless he was very much startled, the odds are he would sneak off through the rhododendrons, without your ever suspecting his presence. In places like the forests on the Black Sea coast, where human beings rarely intrude, you may, it is true, catch him making an early breakfast in the chestnut clumps; but in places like Glola, where he is constantly seeing or hearing human beings, he is as hard to get a shot at as the British wood pigeon.

I was the more annoyed at being able to do nothing at Glola, as I knew that in this part of Radcha the bear that occurs most frequently is the species with the collar mark on the neck, of which I was particularly anxious to get a specimen, the more so as I should like to see whether English naturalists would agree with my friend Dr. Radde that this collared bear is a mere variety of the ordinary brown bear. That the collar is distinctly visible in all ages of the animal I am convinced, having seen specimens from earliest cub-hood to downright old age; and I have the authority of all the Caucasian hunters I ever met for saying that this bear is as different from the ordinary bear in disposition as in coat, being, though a smaller animal, much more dangerous, invariably charging when molested.

Naturally, on arriving at Glola our first business had been to order refreshment for man and beast, and I know nothing more trying than the difficulty of obtaining the merest necessaries at large and prosperous villages, when they are the end of a long journey. The whole of the last long half of your way—hungry, thirsty, and tired—you have been consoling yourself with the thought that however wearisome those last ten versts may be, there is a fixed time at which, if you only persevere, you may slake your thirst and rest your weary limbs. What is the reality? When you have struggled to your goal, you find no house to take you in for some time, no food to buy, for there are no shops or bazaars, and often even the water is a good long step from the village. Then when you have thrown down your things on the bare floor of the beggarly cancellaria, there is no place indoors clean enough to lie down on ; and outside, instead of peace and rest, you are mobbed by a score or two of unclean and inquisitive savages, possessed also of the strongest lungs in the world, who hold long discourses on you, talk to you incessantly, though you don't understand a word, and investigate and play with every article you possess, from your telescope to your toothpick. After enduring this kind of thing for an hour or so, and finding the promises of our numerous friends to bring food unlikely to be fulfilled, I despatched our interpreter to find the starchina, and bring him to me by fair means or foul.

Then I wandered out into the village to see what the peasants' life seemed like here. As it was Sunday, of course all the men were at home and idle, most of them indeed were amusing themselves with a careful investigation of Frank and his belongings on the balcony; and when I came back one of them, a gentleman in a blue shirt, had mounted the table and was delivering a spirited lecture on England and the English, taking my unsuspecting friend for his text. But though none were afield to-day, there was some little work for the women, in the morning and at sundown, to spread out their stores of grain on the threshing floor, casting it like golden motes in the sunbeams, and at night sweeping it up again into its sacks. This done and the cattle tended, the women, like the men, gave themselves to idleness. There was a church in the village, but I saw no one near it, though some grand game heads hung up as votive offerings drew me thither. The whole village indeed, save for our balcony, seemed deserted, and it was not until an hour had slipped away and I went to search for my truant messenger, that I found the reason of this.

A village in Southern Russia is all one long straight street : a village in Radcha or Svânetia has no streets at all, but is a mass of houses huddled together anyhow, between which you squeeze through narrow little alleys, of a thousand windings, over mixens, round the backs of cowsheds, over precipitous stone heaps, to your goal. Winding my way through such a maze as this I came suddenly upon an explanation of the empty houses. At my feet was a boiling little torrent, some twenty or thirty feet wide, with high steep banks, from one to the other of which a single pine trunk formed an uninviting bridge. On the far side a beautiful lawn sloped up into the forest, and half way up it stood a single magnificent walnut tree. Here, with the flickering light and shade playing on them through the leaves overhead, reclined at least half the village, round, alas! a very dirty tablecloth, a heap of cheese, radishes, and chamois flesh, half a dozen great terra cotta jars of wine, and *one* wine glass. There were all the old grey-beards of the village, including the starchina, a large number of picturesquely untidy women, and at the top of the group, by the tree root, my truant interpreter, and a man and woman in European costume. Though I had no fancy for crossing the bridge, I went across and joined the group, being received with tremendous applause, whilst Platon introduced me to his Russian friends, a soldier and his wife staying at Glola, that the woman might go through a course of water cure at its springs.

As soon as I had been settled down into the best place, fresh jars of wine were brought, and with much unction the speech-making and toast-drinking began, while as I did not care for the solids, a little Tcherkess girl got up into the tree and shook me down walnuts for my wine.

In spite of all I have heard of Caucasian female beauty, this girl of twelve was the only really lovely Caucasian I remember to have seen, but she was as beautiful as a dream. As a rule the women seemed to me plain, but then the Mingrelians, whose beauty is most talked of in the Caucasus, are of a thoroughly Hebrew type, which I dislike; and for the others I admit to being unable to see loveliness through an inch and a half of dirt. The sight of the bridge which had to be recrossed, and the memory of my Kutais experiences, soon prevailed over the entreaties of my new friends; and after drinking with half a dozen of the ladies, and getting rid of the unpleasant taste of the rough wine with a long draught of the glorious natural soda water that bubbled up without price and without stint not far from our feet, I made my adieux, and carried off my guide with me to the other side of the stream.

To stay in a place where Platon had found friends, and where I could get no hunters and no dogs, was out of the question; so by dint of never losing sight of him for a moment, I made the unwilling Platon obtain horses before nightfall, and long ere the garrulous inhabitants had asked us half the questions they had to ask we were *en route* for Gebi.

Such a rare night as that on which we rode from Glola to Gebi is enough to soothe even spirits unhinged by haggling with Caucasian horseboys; and though the road was in places dangerously bad, and a puff of hot air like a furnace blast came from time to time from the baked hillsides, marring the evening cool, we still rode on happy through a perfect dream of beauty. For the most part all was dark and wild, like a realisation of one of Doré's pictures; but now and again the moon would seem to sail up from behind some lower peak than usual, and throw flashes of weird, uncertain light on the Rion, rock-bound and raging far below, while at the same time she spread the forest lawns with a cloth of silver, and frosted every trembling leaf with silver light.

High up in the mountains on the other side the Rion we saw from time to time a solitary beacon, embosomed in forest, burning like a ruby on the mountain's breast. From this far-away light came now and again faint echoes of wild unearthly cries, whoopings and whistlings, the ringing of bells and beating of gongs, as if gnomes of the mountain and forest were holding midnight revel there. Could we have looked closer we should have found nothing more supernatural than a wakeful Glola husbandman perched on a raised platform in the middle of the growing maize patch, which he had cultivated amongst the great forest trees, whence (were he not there) the long grey form of old Bruin would steal out every night as the gloaming closed in to rob him of his hard-earned crop. As it is, Bruin knows so well how rarely the husbandman's bullets come near enough to do more than startle him, that he is probably even now at work in some corner where the forest trees cast a shadow, and the sound of his devastations do not reach the watcher's platform.

Further on, where the track passes through a scattered wood of box-trees, on a boulder-studded lawn, we saw a deep pit dug back into the face of a hill, which overlooked the site of a now deserted maize field. Here a year ago another peasant passed many a silent hour (while man was at rest, and only the beasts of the forest roamed the moonlit woodland ways), watching with finger on trigger for the four-footed enemies with whom he had to maintain the struggle for existence. There is no lack of excitement for the farmer here, who, when he has cleared his patch and sown the seed, must guard the produce nightly, or lose all guerdon of his labour.

After passing this hill the way wound down into the bed of the Rion, no longer now the broad peaceful stream, that seems to have grown sluggish and stupid ere it pours its full flood into the Black Sea, nor even the angry, energetic torrent that overthrows all obstacles, and boils onward beneath the grey rocks of Tsess, but a company of half a dozen small streams wandering through a ruinous waste of stony river-bed, over which they unite in winter into a swollen cataract. Here, for the first time, our attention was drawn to large sparks of green light that flew glimmering here and there amongst the birch trees, and it was some time before we realised that they were the first and only fire-flies we had yet seen in the Caucasus.

The last step of the night's march was over a log bridge which spanned the broadest limb of the Rion below Gebi. I venture to think that any English equestrian who was unused to these rough constructions would at first hesitate before crossing at all, and when he did would certainly prefer to cross, if cross he must, on his own feet and not in the saddle. One of our party, Platon, came near to having good cause to regret that he had not done thus; for in spite of the sure-footedness of Caucasian ponies, the holes in this bridge were in such unfair proportion to the solid parts that the poor little quadruped, putting a fore leg through a wide opening, came on his knees and all but rolled over, horse and rider, into the river below.

Of course there were no lights in Gebi. Men in the Caucasus believe that Nature knows best when it is time to work or play and when to sleep, so that the moment the sun is down, unless they are hunting or acting sentinel in their fields, the villagers lie down and sleep until a new day. Groping our way through the houses, our guide stopped us at last with the welcome announcement that we might dismount. We had reached our sleeping quarters.

A perilous ladder, no bad exercise for young climbers, led to the second storey of the cancellaria, where beyond a balcony were two rooms, one of which had rafters to support a floor, but no floor, and the other a floor, perhaps, if one could find it beneath accumulations of varied dirt. The windows were open to the pure night air, or rather the casements were windowless, and the air and rain when there was any was as much at home indoors as without. But there was a table, and in a few minutes Frank had got the tent-bag laid out for a pillow, whilst I took the saddle; and head to tail, side by side, with our boots in dangerous proximity to each other's mouths, we were soon ready for sleep and our insect enemies. But we were premature. Though the village was hushed when we entered it, the news of our arrival roused it, and we soon had the ordinary assembly of sheep-skinned savages shouting round us.

Sheepskins themselves, when worn unwashed for more than three years, are not savoury things to poor European nostrils, but why, oh men of Gebi, why overpower that comparatively innocent smell by the strongest and filthiest of garlic?

Through the first half of the night we were forced to make merry with about a dozen of the elders of the village, who ordered wine to entertain us with, and with that fairness for which they are remarkable emptied the jars and left us to pay for them. They told us the country was alive with game; that not a man amongst them but had slain his thousands and tens of thousands, and the morrow we, too, should kill bears and chamois within a stone's throw of the village. But for all that, when the entertainment was over and our endurance at an end, there was not a single guide forthcoming for the next day, nor even a horse promised to carry our baggage.

The letters which our kind friend, Baron Geikin, had given us to the starchina were, no doubt, powerful and useful in their way, but unluckily there is no law obliging the starchina to keep at home or leave another to perform his duties in his absence, so we never found anyone to present our letters to.

At last, there being no dry place left to expectorate upon, and no more liquor forthcoming, the Elders of Gebi kindly took themselves, their 'makorkha' (a vile kind of rough native tobacco, smoked out of small pipes such as opium-smokers use), and their garlic off to the bosoms of their respective families; and after Platon had cleared decks as well as he was able, we drew our bourkas round us and slept.

When the sun, gleaming in through the roof, woke us out of our heavy slumbers, we entered on another of those vexatious days of bargaining, worry, and procrastination, which take most of the pleasure away from a tour in the Caucasus. Until eleven we could find no one. Then we lost our interpreter, who went to find the starchina. Meanwhile, appetites of English growth began to murmur and rebel at the delay of breakfast, and my half-famished friend and myself made sorties from our stronghold in turn in our endeavours to obtain food.

Unluckily the people of Gebi don't speak Russian, so without Platon we were almost helpless. A quantity of small fowls had an utterly demoralising effect on Frank, and had it not been for extraordinary activity on the part of his intended booty, I am afraid my unfortunate friend would have been guilty of petty larceny at least. But necessity is the mother of invention; and after several abortive attempts, we, by our united efforts, produced an exceedingly striking picture of a cockrel in chalk on a neighbouring wall, after which Frank crowed violently, flapped his coat-tails, went through the pantomime of cutting his own throat, and even of laying an egg; after which he went chuckling about the place like a veritable old hen, until he was purple in the face with his exertions. But our endeavours bore fruit, and before long we had a hatful of eggs, and even a brace and a half of chickens (three for a rouble), and what was even better, learnt the Georgian for these articles of diet for another occasion.

Breakfast over, we got a glimpse at the official life of Gebi. The starchina, accompanied by his secretary, came to visit us, carrying an official document in their hands.

The cancellaria, it seemed, was the starchina's office, in which he transacted all his state affairs. After a considerable search, and some strong language from his chief, who was not quite sober, the secretary managed to find the official seal of the town hidden in a crevice in the wall. From another crevice he produced a tallow candle, a treasure not to be matched this side of Oni, and then came a fierce debate as to where the seal should go. When they had decided that about a dozen impressions should be scattered broadcast over the written part of the document, they appealed to me; and though I daresay they followed out their original plan eventually, for the time being the Elder contented himself by licking paper and seal, holding the latter in the candle-flame for a time, and then making an irregular black mark at the foot of the document as directed by me. After this, the seal and candle were returned to their old hiding places, and tired with the duties of office, the great men took themselves off for a drink.

The office of starchina is awarded by election amongst the members of each village, and the duration of office was, I was told, from three to seven years; but on this head my informants disagreed. As a rule, the office is an unimportant one, as its holder has no real authority, and the members of his village community appear to obey or disobey him pretty much as they please. Moreover, the position is one not greatly sought after, and one of our guides assured me that three roubles' worth of watki judiciously distributed would any day secure the election of the man who gave it.

It would be unkind in me to ask my readers to follow me through the hours of weary haggling, under a scorching sun, to which I had to submit, before horses and men were at last hired; making agreements with men who have no notion of sticking to their contracts, and searching for some glimmerings of truth amongst an ocean of lies to guide me in my search for game. At least half a dozen times I had, after waiting patiently for the advent of promised horses, to go in search of their owners, only to find them round the corner, not dreaming about getting the animals, but eagerly debating with their friends how much more they should demand from me on the next interview. Half a dozen times during the day, with my head aching and tongue dry with talking, I had to plunge my fists up to my elbows into my pockets to keep them from dangerous proximity with the rascals' noses; and then when I had almost choked myself with suppressed vexation, my idiotic interpreter would lose his temper on his own account, upset all my negotiations, and give me all the work to do over again.

Still, when a whole day had been wasted, and even the oldest man was tired of talking, I had got two guides, one of whom had been a bearer in Mr. Freshfield's employ in 1869, and who rejoiced in the name of Vassili, and who, had he not been so devoted to garlic, would have been a very good fellow. The other we unanimously and with great justice entitled 'the duffer.'

As we intended only to make a short excursion to begin with to some tûr-haunted springs of bitter water in the neighbouring mountains, we left our impedimenta in charge of the village priest, and having had a pair of sandals apiece manufactured by our gillies, and received Platon's assurance that he had laid in all necessary supplies of creature comforts, we left Gebi for the first time about five o'clock on the evening of August 21.

CHAPTER IV.

KEERTEESHO.

For our journey to Keerteesho, where the mineral springs were, we were told we could get no horses, and as the guides talked of its being forty versts from Gebi, Frank and myself started up the first hill outside the town with a feeling that hard times were going to begin in real earnest, and if the guides could honestly walk forty versts a day in such country as this, we had better give up all idea of attempting to do as they did.

For the first day or two of our seven or eight weeks' tramping in the Caucasus my friend suffered a good deal from walking in sandals, becoming very footsore all at once, and remaining so for a considerable time ; but to me during the whole time, and to him as soon as his feet had hardened, these rough hay-padded mocassins were inexpressibly easy and useful. To attempt to climb grass slopes on the mountain sides without them would appear to me madness, for while nails in your boots make a noise and slide off every smooth rock, your sandals are so thin and pliant that your foot can grip the hillsides like a hand, and your tread is as noiseless as a cat's. The sandal in use here, by the way, is laced along the bottom, so as to give a better grip.

Our path to-night ran along the side of a chain of wooded hills, from which we caught glimpses of Gebi and the river, set in a frame of leafy boughs, from time to time. As we left the town further and further behind us, we began to come upon small clearings, patches of corn, and groups of those villagers whose absence had made the town behind us seem so deserted. Half a dozen times we came upon little parties of peasant women going back in the gloaming to the village, and so timid were they that, though our guides called to them by name and assured them of our harmlessness, they bounded like wild things down the hillside as soon as they caught sight of us, and did not even stay to stand and gaze before they had put a very considerable start between themselves and the strangers.

Just now the forests and mountains seemed more full of people than the village streets, for every one who can work is afield during the short summer months, unless they would with their families starve during the nine months' winter. When we passed through the district it was the season of barley harvest, and in every clearing were bevies of girls at work with the reaping hook, singing while they reaped, while not a few of them stopped from time to time to take a look at or talk to the dirty little brat whose long, wooden cradle they had carried from Gebi to the field in the morning, and who now lay by its mother's side as she worked. Not far off in case of need the husband was doing his share of the harvest, with his long rifle slung from a bough close to his hand; and busy though he seemed, it would be a lucky chamois who should pass in sight of those grey crags the other side the valley without calling the peasant from husbandry to the chase.

When we had done about eight versts roughish walking, and the evening had begun to close in, our guide turned aside into a basin of cornfields among the forest trees, and informed us that one of the wigwams of boughs before us was to be our camp for the night. Eight versts seemed a shamefully short march for a day's work, but somehow no one mur-

mured. Our hut was a circular structure of bent boughs put together when still green in the early summer, with all their foliage left on. By the tent pole in the centre were a few slabs of slate, and here we soon built up a fire, that lit up the interior with a ruddy glow, and kept us constantly employed picking up sparks which shot right and left into our bedding of dry fern and hay, which was massed up round the wall of our wigwam. It seemed as if the whole thing must be in a blaze every moment; but this feeling soon went off, and, though we were cooking our last chicken, we felt no foreboding. While leaning back in our scented couches we listened to peasants singing somewhere in the woods above us, and gave ourselves up to laziness and tobacco.

After supper we took our rifles and strolled out round the edges of the cornfields, in the hope that somewhere where the forest threw its darkest shadows we might find a bear had crept silently into the barley; but alas! the moon lit up every nook and corner, and everywhere fires were burning, and the loquacious reapers chattering and singing. On our way back we tried to overcome the shyness of some of the wood nymphs we met, and made an effort at conversation with them. But it was no good. Though they wanted a light for their fire and cigarettes they would only consent to take it when thrown to them, and, having secured the ember, scampered away laughing to where a low branch hut just showed a few feet above some still uncut corn.

Beautiful as the night was, we had to be up by dawn on the morrow, and if our guides were to be believed, we had still eighty-two versts to tramp before our goal was reached, so we left the cornfields to the reapers and the bears, and turned in to roost.

Some time, about an hour before dawn, we

woke with a shiver, for these clearings are too near the glaciers to be ever very warm at night, and, tossing on fresh logs to the dying fire, sent such a shower of bright sparks up to our now dry roof, that before we knew where we were the whole edifice was beginning to burn. Thanks to our exertions—chiefly Frank's, I think—we stopped the fire before it had done much more than burn out some of our ceiling, and nothing else happened to disturb us until our interpreter informed us it was time to be moving.

One of the most useful of the small necessaries we had brought with us was half a dozen books of the 'feuilles de savon,' patented, I fancy, by some German for the use of travellers. A soap-leaf by the river's brim was with us the ordinary prelude to a day's work, after which our mocassins were dredged up from the bottom of a pool, in which they had been soaking; and after being filled with 'tommy' (short mountain grass), were put on dripping over a pair of stockings, which had been carefully dried before the camp fire during the night. I think it was a kind of superstition with us; for whatever else we neglected, we rarely if ever failed to keep a pair of dry stockings handy, although we invariably had them soaking wet ten minutes after we put them on, and kept them so all day.

One of life's mysteries to me is, why should damp feet in England invariably bring upon me colds, rheumatism, and all the ills that flesh is heir to, while in the Caucasus I never went dry shod, waded a dozen times a day nearly waist deep through streams of ice-water fresh from its parent glacier, slept even in wet things, and yet never suffered from any ill effect. Amongst the peasants, too, and hunters, none ever wear any other foot covering than the sandal, are everlastingly wet, treating mountain rivulets knee-deep with absolute indifference, are innocent of umbrellas and waterproofs, and yet are untouched by colds or rheumatism.

Breakfast time this morning brought with it a terrible revelation for my poor friend, to whom meat seemed an absolute necessity. Our interpreter had trusted implicitly to our guide's assurances that we should bag game before nightfall, and the wretched little fowl which we had crucified in the flames last night was the only scrap of meat in camp, so that we had to be content with maize-bread and water for breakfast, Platon having left our kettle behind, as well as other stores.

From about seven until two we followed the course of the little river Tchosura along the base of wooded hills, in which the clearings became rarer and rarer as we proceeded, until about a couple of versts before crossing the Dombouri—a feat performed on a single pine pole—they ceased altogether. By daylight we could see that every field of grain was traversed in every direction by bear tracks, and all along our path were signs of their presence and the ravage they committed on the crops; but to look for the bears in the daytime, in the dense jungle which bordered our path, would have been a hopeless affair.

At last, about 2 P.M., when our ever up hill path had reached an elevation of 2,000 feet above sea level, and we had already arrived in a *cul-de-sac* of grey rocks, backed and ended by a great glacier descending from a range of snow peaks in front of us, whence rose the river Tchosura, our guide Vassili stopped on a certain grassy knoll, and having lighted his pipe and seated himself, whistled loud and long.

Before the whistle was well ended, our party received an addition in the form of a tall well-knit man of Radcha, clad in garments of many patches, whose face, rags, and rifle all proclaimed him shepherd and sportsman perhaps, but certainly sportsman. He was the genius of the place, the man to whom each quaint branch shanty belonged, who had made the camp under the pine we had passed *en route*, who had lived and hunted here so much that the men of Gebi had almost got to look on Keerteesho as Simon's property. And he was no bad lord of such a wild domain. Tall and light built, with a steady blue eye that looked you straight in the face, his long lithe limbs seemed as if there was no crag in the mountains round to which they could not bear their owner. And his reputation matched his looks. In all Radcha there is no hunter like the hunter of Keerteesho, and Simon is his name; and I may add here that though he had a few faults, like other men, he was the finest Caucasian peasant I ever saw, and the best servant and friend we met in our travels.

When we had shaken hands and learnt that the starchina had refused to let Simon apply for a berth as guide and hunter with us, and had instead given us one of his underlings, who admitted readily that he had never killed anything larger than that liveliest of insects, we at once appointed Simon hunter-in-chief, and made 'the duffer' pack-horse to the expedition. We then suggested to Simon the propriety of lunching, but though he had over fifty cattle in the hills around, he could offer us nothing better than a mess of boiled beans in a broken wooden bowl, which he had been reserving for his own dinner. Unluckily for us, whilst we were at Gebi all true believers were keeping a very important fast; and these poor fellows, in spite of their hard work, were supporting life in the keen mountain air on bread and water.

Having lunched just sufficiently to realise how hungry we were, we sent 'the duffer' back there and then to Gebi, with orders to return as soon as possible with meat and wine, after which we rose and followed Simon up a steeper ascent than ever to the quarters he had mentally assigned to us. An hour and a half or two hours' walking and climbing by goats' tracks up the steep hillside, brought us to where a huge blackened stone projected into the path, and here our guide dropped his load and sat down with the air of a man who had reached his own hall door.

A peep beyond the big stone revealed a tiny cave, in which perhaps four men and a fire might be packed, if each took up the least space possible and no one minded getting singed. Here the blackened roof, the bedding of old straw, some game bones, and a couple of broken pitchers, clearly indicated a favourite haunt of Simon's; and in these cramped quarters, a fire having been lit, Frank and I were soon installed with our interpreter. The men and our host were to sleep outside, there being no room for them with us. But we were not allowed much rest even here. The sun was now getting low in the heavens, and Simon felt fully assured that ere his setting a mountain sheep should die. So having left our loads at the cave we began again our upward course, until we wound out on to the edge of a steep cleft in one of the chief peaks, on which Simon had built him an eyrie, fenced in with great boulders, masked with currant bushes and carpeted with hay. From here you obtained a view of the chief object of attraction to the tûr for miles around.

High up on a bare face of grey rock, between the two walls of the ravine, was a bright yellow stain, where a spring of iron water welled constantly over the brim of a little natural cup in the rock. To this, from the dizziest of the white heights above, three thread-like lines seemed to trend, worn by the feet of mountain sheep, from year to year in places which would give anything but a mountain sheep vertigo to look at. One of these paths, the lowest, was commanded by our eyrie, and on this we all fixed our gaze intently for the next few hours.

Round us nothing seemed to grow but a few bilberries, but lower down we had passed through deep beds of blue larkspur, broken off and seen our companions eat the seed pods of great tiger lilies, and almost lost sight of each other amongst the tall stems of a white umbelliferous flower unfamiliar to me. Over the heads of the flowers now and then flitted a clouded yellow, and not once or twice, but several times, I saw the grand hovering flight of an Apollo, a flight which always struck me as the strongest and most hawk-like among butterflies. I used often to watch these fine fellows poising like a wind-hover over the wild flowers, but any attempt to catch them only demonstrated to me more plainly that I had not the wings of an Apollo, and up-hill a welter weight had no chance with a butterfly. Besides the Apollos there were two or three kinds of white butterflies, which were not like any English species—one a kind of wood white I think, another which might have been the Bath white, and a third larger than any white I know; but of this I only saw or thought I saw two specimens, and they were not very near.

Meanwhile the evening has come upon us, and it is getting almost too dark to see, when suddenly Simon, who has been absent over an hour, clutches my arm and silently signs to me to follow him. Out of the eyrie we sneak through a few azalea bushes, until we get behind the brow of the hill, and then Simon simply takes straight up-hill as if the devil was at his heels. Thanks to a love of boxing and other athletic exercises I am never in very bad wind, but ten minutes (or it may have been only five) of such a scamper simply leaves me breathless. Unable to make myself understood I clutch at my guide's skirts and sign to him to go slower. The look of indignant surprise and pity he bestows on me is rather worse than a knock-down blow, but thank heaven he does go a trifle slower for a while. To him, knowing every stone on the hillside, it is all very well, but for me I have been putting my feet down recklessly and in ignorance ever since I started. Poor Frank put his arm out on the way to the eyrie, though thanks to luck and experience he got it in again almost at once, and the way to the eyrie was as a high road compared to this *viâ diabolica*.

At last Simon sees I can go no further, and signing to me to sit down on a spot to which it requires all the energies of ten trembling fingers to cling to keep my position, disappears into the darkness above. Then I sit and wait for what seems hours, wondering if this hunter of Radcha intends me to remain extended for ever, a modern Prometheus, on these Caucasian rocks. To get down by myself in the darkness from my present perch seems out of the question, and night spent there almost equally so.

At last I hear a shot, and some few minutes after Simon comes skipping and sliding down alongside me, as if he were merely descending the mound in Greenwich Park. The light had been too bad for him to make sure of his shot, but he had got very near and believed he had wounded a tûr, a surmise confirmed on inspection next morning; for though we never bagged the poor beast, the stones were red with its blood.

On our way back to the cave we heard showers of stones come rattling down from the rocks around us, as another herd came down to drink; but it was too dark even for Simon to climb now, and far too dark to shoot, so we let them drink in peace, and went back to our supper of bread and water with an appetite that even made such poor fare palatable.

Thanks to my restless friend, the impossibility of arranging myself on the uneven boulders that formed my bed, and Simon's thousands of insect retainers, I slept but little that night, and was not very sorry when I was turned out into the starlight to climb up to our ambuscade once more. This time no tûr came, they had all drunk in the dark hours of the night, and had now taken themselves back to their haunts in the dizzy peaks above, so we had our vigil for nothing.

One of the peculiarities of Keertcesho was the want of bird-life. In a bush near us I watched for awhile a pair of (I think) mountain accentors, and once I saw a pair of rock pigeons far away below us, while on the way up I recognised once or twice the droppings of black game; but save for these I saw no sign of bird life nor heard any note.

The worst of this system of watching for tûr at their drinking-place or 'lick' is that the sportsmen must keep out of sight and quiet all day, for once let some wily old veteran sight a man in the vicinity of his haunts and not a tûr will come near the spring for a day or two.

When the vigil of the morning was over, we could only creep away back to our cave, and there wile away the time as best we might until four o'clock came round again. We had now had two days' fasting on bread and water, when towards noon we caught sight of 'the duffer' toiling up to our camp well laden with chickens and a skin of wine. The reception he met with was enthusiastic, and we all got to work at once to prepare a feast.

Our cooking utensils were of a primitive order—one blackened earthenware pot, in which we boiled one diminutive fowl at a time, and a broken wooden cup, from which we drank the soup in turns. But though rough they served our turn, and being refreshed we began to think of preparing a more comfortable abode for ourselves than the smoky little bear's den, with its blackened boulders and cramped accommodation. But it was no good. There was not a level place on which to pitch our tent apparently nearer than Gebi. So we had to give it up.

All day long our men sat smoking and cleaning their rifles, and a wilder or more picturesque group than they made it would be hard to imagine, in their sheepskin turbans, brown cloth gaiters, sandals, canvas shirts and long togas originally of a rock brown, but now so patched with cloths of every hue—red, brown, yellow, and grey—that it would be hard to find much of the original material left ; yet all the colours blend so well and are so quaintly like the lichen-covered, iron-stained rocks around, that it is not easy to beat them as stalking costumes.

Two or three beads and a charm hang round each wild fellow's neck ; at his waist is a belt with flint and steel, dagger, gun-screw, bullet extractor, and every other necessary gunner's tool. Everything else that his simple wants require is to be found in the breast of his shirt; and the proverbial schoolboy's pocket would not compare for variety of contents with a Caucasian shirt front. Tobacco-pouch and pipe, lumps of rock-salt to eat with his beans, dried galls of mountain sheep to cure every ailment to which he is subject, bullets, matches, tinder, and a score of other odds and ends are produced as they are wanted from this inexhaustible store-room. That his coat is ragged is small wonder, for, apart from the ravages of the rocks, every time he loads or cleans his rifle he tears off a strip from his coat-tails, and every wound that wants stanching is supplied with a bandage from the same quarter.

All three of our men have all the hair shaved close off their heads, and one of the amusements of the day was to sharpen a pocket-knife of mine and shave each other, a process more sanguinary than successful. None of the four seem in the least degree to consider themselves as servants; but even the worst of them was always ready to serve us, and give up the best of everything for our use, while Simon's watchfulness and motherly care for our safety became almost oppressive.

Towards afternoon there was a great palaver amongst the men, and after much discussion, Simon and Vassili gave me to understand that I was to follow them to the highest of the watch-stations, to which none of us had ascended as yet, while Frank kept guard below.

I have seldom had such a disagreeable climb as that first ascent to 'the nest,' as we called it, and though, before I left the mountains, I should not have thought much of doing it alone, my grip of Simon's coat-tails was uncommonly tight as I went up for the first time. However, thanks to these and Vassili's stalwart shoulder propping me up from below, I made a safe, albeit undignified ascent, stopping to take a draught of the mineral water at the tûr's lick on the way.

The spring bubbles up in a tiny natural cup, and is so strongly impregnated with iron that two or three mouthfuls are as much as you can swallow. Both my guides drank of it greedily, alleging that it gave strength and renewed health to the drinker.

'The nest' was a mere ledge high up on the bare face of the cliff, with no apparent way up or down ; a bit of rock jutting out above sheltered it from the rain, and a small collection of boulders on the outer edge fenced it in and hid its inmates from sight, leaving perhaps three feet in width by seven in length, on which Simon and I had to dispose ourselves for the night. It was a wild bed, and the less you looked over the edge into the precipice below, and calculated on the chance of tossing in your sleep the better you liked it ; but regrets were useless, and as I watched Vassili scrambling down to safer sleeping quarters, I felt I was a fixture until broad daylight came again. Neither Simon nor I spoke. We could not make each other understand if we wanted to, and besides, as we watched the light fade, and the stars come out and glisten on the riven snow peaks, so little higher than ourselves, a silence came down upon us that no doubt he felt, as I did, it would be sacrilege to break.

Presently, when the night fully set in, and there was no longer any chance of the túr coming until the morning, my companion dusted away a few of the biggest of the stones from my couch, rolled up his coat as a pillow for my head, and curled my bourka round my feet. Then he went to the edge, and standing with his hat off, looking above the highest peaks, his lips moved silently for a few minutes, and as the silver starlight lit up the stern weather-worn features and keen earnest eyes, I could not help thinking that man's faith, whatever it was, seemed worthy of his surroundings. Of course I gave him back his coat, and as nothing on earth would stop his smoking, lit my own pipe, too, before I turned in. 'If the wind is right for you,' Simon always insisted, 'a pipe will do no harm, and if wrong for you, then abstinence from the beloved weed can do no good.' So he always smoked, and I believe lost me many a good head by doing so.

A bourka (Caucasian blanket) is a wonderful thing for warmth, and once wound round you, so as to exclude the air, you can keep warm in the coldest night. On this particular night, even my stony couch could not keep me awake, and it was only at intervals, when my gillie roused me, that I learnt what was happening round us.

Twice, as we listened, showers of small stones came rattling down from the peaks above. Then there would be a long pause. Again a rattling of stones, and then a sharp 'djik, djik,' half whistle, half bleat. Two or three herds came to drink in the night, though towards midnight a storm broke over the mountains, giving us glimpses of the peaks around standing out black and stern in a pale flood of lightning.

For a time the storm seemed exactly overhead, and the big rain drops splashed off our protecting rock above in a way that made us crouch closer under its kindly shelter; then it passed away, and for nearly an hour afterwards we could hear it moaning and rattling among the distant peaks.

Then we slept again until about 3 A.M. I suppose, when I once more felt Simon's grip upon my arm. Now it was no longer night, but a dim shadowy light, in which a few weird rock shapes were indistinctly visible, and the stars were getting white in the heaven.

All round us the clatter of stones was incessant, and the sharp calls of the mountain sheep were close and frequent on all sides, while the bleating of the young kids told us plainly that a large herd was drinking close to us. But strain our eyes as we would not even Simon could see anything of our visitors for nearly half an hour. At last he made one out as the bleating grew less frequent, and the stones had almost ceased to rattle. Following his directions I, too, made out what seemed like the grey ghosts of two goats rapidly disappearing into the clouds on the other side; and, obeying his directions, though I could not hope to hit, I fired right and left at what he afterwards told me were two young kids, the last of the herd, slowly following their impatient dam into the safer heights.

I suppose I ought to have felt disgusted at my night's fruitless watch, but I am afraid I didn't, forgiving myself even for my miss, and watching the waves of mist, driven like white smoke through the green and grey rocks, with a pleasure that the consideration of an unnecessarily prolonged stay in our nest by no means destroyed. At length it cleared sufficiently for us to find our way down to our comrades, who had had no better luck than ourselves.

Lying that morning, after breakfast, outside our cave, we made out on the ridge beyond the Tchosura a large herd of chamois feeding and playing in a hollow of the hills, which the morning sun had not yet penetrated. Tired of so much inaction as we had been doomed to for the last three days, I at once proposed that we should attempt to stalk them; but to this my guides gave a decided negative, at least for the present, so that I had to content myself with watching the bonny beasts through my glass.

At last the sun crept into the hollow and banished the cool shadows, whereupon the whole herd left off playing and feeding, and one by one lay down in the tall herbage. None of them seemed easily pleased with their lairs, for, after lying for some time with their heads held well up, they would rise and take a steady stare all round, after which they again lay down. At last, however, they were all at rest, and Simon shut his glass with an energy that meant the first act was over.

The chief difficulty was the river, over which there was no bridge for miles, and to wade which all, except Simon, said was impossible. By dint of coaxing and determination, I eventually wrought on Simon (who was the only really keen sportsman among them) to make the attempt. Frank decided not to come with us, but to try later on for bears.

Down at the river's edge the rough water, whose depth we had not yet fathomed, frightened Vassili into a determined refusal to have anything to do with our venture. Remembering a very nearly fatal ducking I had once before in a Caucasian torrent, I myself did not feel too keen for the plunge, but Simon had me by the hand now, and we were in for it together. It was terribly strong and deep, that source of the Tchosura, and the way it surged and swept round its great boulders, wetting us above our waists, was the reverse of reassuring. Besides, it was cold as death. But we kept a good grip of each other's hands, and struggled safe to shore to stamp the water out of our sandals, and laugh at the rueful face of our friend upon the further shore. My gallant Simon soon plunged in again, and for a moment, as he and Vassili staggered about in mid-stream, blundering amongst the big boulders, I was afraid I should have to wade back alone. If they had lost their footing, as they so nearly did, I should have been powerless to help them, but as good luck would have it, they just managed to right themselves in time.

Crossing these little mountain rapids costs many a good man's life in the Caucasus, and one of the best of servants, my poor Stepan, who served me faithfully at Golovinsk, some four years ago, met his death in a rapid he and I have probably waded together a score of times. Poor fellow! he was very rough and untaught, but an unselfish good servant to me for all that.

Once over the stream, our way was easy enough. The bed of a winter torrent afforded us a road, stony and toilsome indeed, but by no means difficult. That we were not the only passengers by it, numerous bear-tracks, broken raspberry canes, and other signs made very manifest, but the wayfarers whose tracks we saw move about very little, except at night, so we saw nothing of them.

When we had reached the spot at which I expected to sight the chamois, Simon crept on ahead through the thick rhododendron bushes, and after an absence of a few minutes, came back saying we had had our climb for nothing. The game had moved on. Hoping to find the chamois at no great distance, we pushed carelessly through the rattling scrub, when, just as we reached the edge of a small precipice, the sound of loosened boulders bounding away into the valley below drew our attention, and there, a hundred yards below us, roused by our presence from their noon-day siesta, was the whole herd going as hard as they could lay legs to the ground, bounding over rocks and boulders as if they were furnished with wings rather than legs.

I suppose some of those who read this have missed a running deer before to-day, so they at least won't be hard on me, as those might who have only fired at marks. After all my trouble, I missed right and left, starring the rock with both barrels a few inches over my game.

I don't know what other men think about it, but to my mind an 'Express' rifle is by no means the best weapon for running shots, and for the future I am mightily tempted to use a smooth-bore with no back sight to bother me. If your beast will only remain stationary for a few seconds, nothing can touch an Express; and in self-defence I may say that I have always made really good shooting with it under such circumstances, but I have, I am afraid, yet to learn how to shoot snap shots with my favourite weapon. I always shoot high.

After this failure sadness came down on me like a cloud, and as I sat munching bilberries and listening to the long shrill whistle of the evil little beasts who had eluded me, now half way into the next province, I came to the conclusion that Keerteesho was an unlucky encampment, and the sooner we made a fresh start the better.

On arriving in camp, I found Frank had also had an unsuccessful cruise, having found quantities of fresh bear tracks and one lair only just deserted, but no bears. This being the case, it was not hard to induce him to see with my eyes ; and next morning we were *en route* for Gebi again, doing the distance back in rather less than half the time we took coming—a by no means singular incident in this country, where the road out is invariably represented as three times longer than it really is.

CHAPTER V.

SHUKACHÂLO.

WHEN we came back to Gebi, empty-handed and crestfallen, we felt far too humble to resent the sneers of those local Nimrods who had bade us go forth certain to return in a day or two laden with the *spolia opima* of the mountains. To our surprise, instead of contempt we met with universal sympathy, and in answer to our oft repeated, 'Never killed anything all the week,' the simple faces of those who had told us of the largest bags made daily within a mile or two of Gebi, beamed a cheerful, 'Well, there's nothing very wonderful in that!' But as we began to know the men of this country better we understood these things; for, in spite of the quantity of game round Gebi and the much vaunted prowess of the hunters of that mighty city, so bad are their guns and so indifferent their shooting, that the return of a hunter other than empty-handed becomes at once one of the events of the year.

But though far from truthful, the men of Radcha are hospitable souls, and having left the wretched cancellaria, round which the odour of Vassili's garlic still clung, we made ourselves comfortable at the village priest's, and received the guests who came trooping in to see us there. First there was the priest himself, proud possessor of the only two glasses in Gebi and sole owner of a real teapot. The possession of these articles alone, and his knowledge of a little Russian, raised him at once to a stratum of civilisation which the humble men of Gebi regard with pride and respect. Having duly admired these wonders of civilisation we proceeded to make use of them, while about every five minutes a fresh arrival brought us some trifling offering for our feast.

Simon, the ragged and unkempt, returned after about half an hour's absence, clean shaved, in a bright red shirt and nearly new tcherkesska, with a big brass chain hanging across his manly bosom and a look of conscious pride and self-respect on his face that would have become a churchwarden. Better than all, he was the bearer of three immense cheese cakes and a jug of milk from his wife, which, together with a host of other supplies, were provided gratuitously for our entertainment.

Poor Simon and Vassili had to content themselves with a mess of beans and bread, but our interpreter Platon, disregarding the mandates of his religion, treated the fast with contempt, and joined heartily in our supper. His friends and co-religionists of Gebi, instead of appearing shocked at the laxity of his religious principles, seemed to admire him as a being of superior culture, for whom of course the laws concerning feasts and fasts were not meant to be so binding as they were for themselves.

After supper we had to go seriously into money matters, and we were obliged to yield to the unpleasant conviction that unless we could obtain money at once we should have to return to Kutais. It seemed a risky thing at first sight to trust our interpreter with any large sum, but there was no other way out of our difficulty; and to go back to Kutais, to be stifled by the heat and driven mad by the difficulties of making a fresh start, was not to be thought of. So we gave him thirty pounds in circular notes and letters to some friends of ours, and having secured his native passport and most of his clothes under the pretext of taking care of them for him, we made arrangements for him to leave Gebi for Kutais next morning, to return in a week's time, and rejoin us at our camp beneath the glacier of Lapûr.

The next thing to be thought of was the means of communication with our guides in his absence, as there is always a chance of the language of signs breaking down before the end of a week, and the rest of the evening I spent in collecting a vocabulary of the Georgian words most likely to be of everyday occurrence. This done, I turned in and slept long and soundly, until the crowing of cocks and a continued droning sound in the court-yard below the balcony woke me to a sense that Sunday morning had come, and the fifteen days' fast of the death of the Holy Virgin was ended.

The droning under the balcony was an

early morning service being conducted by my host the priest, who in his shirt sleeves stood bare-headed beneath the ladder which led to our room, and intoned, I believe, a species of liturgy to a congregation of two at a pace which no clergyman of the Church of England could hope to rival. His congregation must have known their prayers uncommonly well if they recognised any of them at that railroad speed.

When the service was over, our host came up to us and brought us a parcel which had arrived for us from our friend Baron Geikin, containing a present of a bottle of liqueur, some tobacco, and other luxuries.

After writing a note of thanks to the Baron, we started Platon off with it, and went down to the river to try if we could see any trout rising, as the priest assured us that he frequently caught a nice basket of fish close to the town by a primitive kind of 'daping.' However, I was as unlucky here as elsewhere in the Caucasus, never having seen a trout rise during the whole of my autumn campaign.

As we strolled up from the river Gebi presented a different aspect from that which it wore a week ago. Then all the streets were still, all the houses empty save for a few old crones long past the possibility of work. Now at every street corner men less ragged than usual were loafing, laughing and smoking, while troops of women in bright coloured garments and gaudy turbans were sitting on the house ladders, or hurried chattering through the town. But in spite of all the merry making, Simon the hunter was waiting for us when we got home, to tell us that if we would engage a half-starved looking creature, whom he called nephew, as horseboy, the said nephew would act as interpreter for us, and have horses ready for a start that night.

I very soon found that Deto's only claim to being a Russian scholar was the possession of a ragged old Russian uniform which he wore, and a lively memory of a Russian term of abuse, no doubt often applied to himself. These were hardly good qualifications for an interpreter, but to please Simon, Frank and I engaged the fellow; and towards evening he came to us with a raw-boned old mare and her foal, with which for our baggage animals we started for Lapûr and Svânetia—not a very imposing expedition to look at, as we trudged out of Gebi, the foal making occasional attempts to bolt for some tempting pasture to our right or left, attempts which Deto and Simon did all they knew to frustrate, while the old mare, laden with a large black kettle, our saddle-bags and guns, formed the centre of the main party.

On our way out of the town we passed one of the strangest scenes it has ever been my lot to behold. Just where the houses cease and the valley of the Rion begins again, stands one of the regulation green and white Russian churches, not a large or gorgeous edifice by any means, but about the best in Radcha. Round this on Sunday evening was a circle of fires, and on every fire a caldron, such as (only larger than) the caldron commonly supposed to have been used by the witches in the incantation scene in 'Macbeth.'

Round each fire squatted a crowd of such wild and loquacious beings as can only be found by the banks of the Rion, while between and about the caldrons were huge piles of raw meat, the mortal remains of nine bullocks slain to keep the feast which follows on the fast of the death of the Virgin. Seven of these bullocks were a present from the municipal body of the town, the other two beasts were provided by subscription ; nine bullocks being considered necessary to feed the hungry

PERSIAN GIPSY MUSICIANS.

inhabitants of the 140 houses which go to make up Gebi. In the pots were seething huge messes of tripe and other tid-bits, of which a burly cook offered us a sample on the end of a huge trident. Nor were the kindly fellows content to let us leave them in their feasting without something to cheer us on our way, but insisted on our men carrying off a portion to consume later on.

When all those gathered round the caldrons have fed to repletion, the remnant of the feast is divided amongst the heads of houses, according to the number of souls in each family, so that before night every morsel has been cleared away. If they were as other men are, what an opportunity there would be for Cockle or Eno during the next fortnight; but as it is there are no doctors in Radcha, nor any quacks, therefore perhaps indigestions are unimpaired and appetites enormous.

For half a mile down the river a little

band of followers came with us to speed the parting guests, and then we were left to ourselves, silently plodding on into the quiet glens of the mountains that separate Radcha from Svânetia.

Just before the gloaming a whistle echoed shrilly through the glen, and a tall shepherd came racing down from some hut hidden in the woods which clothed the slope above us. By the kiss of greeting which he gave Simon we concluded he was some relative of his, and that he was a good fellow we felt certain when, doffing his shako of sheepskin, he presented us with a huge bowl of curds and whey. To devour this at our leisure we retired to a little fern-hung dell, where a bright mountain stream sparkled up from a bed of moss, and here at our guide's suggestion put down our burdens and ate our evening meal.

All round was absolutely silent: no harvest cries came from the corn-lands, no birds' voices broke the woodland silence, and by our guides' movements, as well as by their conversation, I knew that game was not far off. Now I admit I don't like shooting on Sunday. It may be a puerile superstition—and I fear I can give no very valid reason why one should not as soon shoot as travel on that day—but we are all of us creatures of habit and impulse, and on this evening in particular I didn't wish to break my rule. However, the temptation was too strong for me, and when the evening had fairly closed in and my men had at last loaded their ancient fire-arms satisfactorily, Frank and Vassili took one line and Simon and I another, pushing our way up hill through the belt of woods, until we gained a kind of tableland or ridge, where between two belts of forest trees a long waving line of yellow corn-fields caught the last light of the August evening.

For two evenings now no noise of men or

light of fires had broken the solitude of the place, and it was Simon's hope that this peaceful state of things would induce cautious old Michael to forget his usual prudence and come out openly before nightfall to feed among the crops. Here and there among the cornfields were little clumps of forest, or fragments of dark rock, and now and again you came upon patches of corn which seemed to have wandered within the dark circle of the great trees and become islanded and imprisoned there. Here it was that we crept about with most silent steps, conscious that no more fitting supper-room could be fashioned by nature for our prey than these dim and silent corners.

We had just topped a long swell of cornland; and having convinced myself, in spite of the waning light, that all the charred and blackened stumps which stood among the corn were stumps indeed, and were not in motion, I was enjoying the broad bands of cinnamon-coloured cloud in which the dark peaks of the distant mountains seemed floating islands, when Simon dragged me down on my knees with the single word 'arrees' ('there's one!'). One look was enough at Simon's face, working with intense excitement, and then trusting entirely to him I forbore to gratify my own eyes, but slunk away on hands and knees until we were well below the level of the little hill from which my man had viewed the game.

Not far from where we were was one of the forest islands I have alluded to, from which a long peninsula of dark trees stretched out towards the point at which the bear was feeding. Going at a run we were soon in its shadow, and in a few minutes more were peering over a huge boulder at the long tawny shape that looks so different moving silently in the shadow of its native forests from the poor spiritless beasts who disgrace the name of Bruin in the Zoo.

From where we were we could not hear him as he moved, nor was he in the least degree conscious of our presence, and I would gladly have watched him longer, but Simon was boiling over with impatience, and the bear was feeding every second more and more into the shadow. So I tried to balance my rifle on Simon's alpenstock for a rest, and though I could not see my foresight clearly, aimed low and pulled trigger. Not for the first time since I have begun bear-shooting did I become conscious of the fact that with a quick swing of his huge body my old enemy had galloped off without a sound into the forest, apparently untouched. Whether he was hit or not I don't know—he evidently was not very badly hurt; and owing to the bad light I felt very little confidence in my shooting and did not attempt to follow him, though I have known a bear take a mortal wound without a whimper and go off as if nothing had happened.

Simon was not so angry as I expected, and seemed to think he had over-rated my rifle's powers, and to be resolved another time to get me as near as he would require to be himself. That night we saw no more bears, but twice during the night we heard the echoes rattling amongst the hills in answer to Frank's rifle far away at the other end of the table-land. Gradually it grew too dark to see, and then we left the fields, and after half an hour's scrambling and sliding in the dark, we saw the light of our camp fire glimmer up from the meadow by the river's edge through the last fringe of the lower belt of woods. There was no time then for building up a 'palagan' (hut of boughs) or erecting our tent, so we piled up our log fire to enormous dimensions, rolled ourselves in our bourkas, and prepared to make a night of it, '*sub Jove frigido.*'

Frank came in soon after us with a tale like our own of wasted opportunities. His first shot had been a lucky one, equally distant from himself and his guide, the result of the accidental discharge of the abominably constructed 'Peabody' with which he was handicapped. The second shot had been at a bear which he and Vassili had met at fairly close quarters, but which, thanks to the dark, escaped with nothing worse than a bad frightening. We ought, perhaps, to have been sad, and held ourselves as of very small account for the way we had let our bears off, but I am afraid all proper sense of shame was dead in us; so we blamed the twilight, blamed the rifles, blamed anything except ourselves, and blessing the man who first taught the use of tobacco, looked hopefully forward to another day at the deserted corn-fields on the morrow.

About 1 A.M., when the camp fire was dying out and our sleep was at its soundest, a party of shepherds from Gebi arrived on the scene, and with that glorious want of ceremony that characterises their race, woke us out of our slumbers and re-lit the fire. All they wanted, good simple souls, was a chat, and it never occurred to them that we should not see things from their point of view. It is no good getting in a rage when you can't make yourself understood, so I made the best of it, and I was rewarded for my forbearance by being allowed to go to sleep again in about half an hour's time.

The last I saw of them was a glimpse of five or six forms in sheepskins squatting round the fire and smoking, without apparently any idea of going to sleep that night. Next morning, though I was up by daylight, shepherds and flocks had gone, and left no trace behind them.

As it was no good going into the cornfields until evening, we determined to try the spur of mountains at whose foot we were camped for chamois. Frank and Vassili took the low end of the spur, while Simon and I climbed the higher part at the other end, intending to meet about the middle.

The climb through the forest to the top of the ridge was about as severe exercise as any man would care to take, for, in addition to the constant steepness of the ascent, the undergrowth was so luxuriant as to entirely stop the way from time to time. These enforced halts were seized on eagerly by Simon to collect currants, raspberries, the young seed pods of the great lilies, and half-a-dozen other things which these men eat.

All through and through the tangle of weeds and brush ran bear slides, places down which old Michael had slithered when he left his lair to seek the fruit bushes of the valley.

By-and-bye we came to a dark corner, where, high up, just above the belt of wood on the edge of a watercourse, a big rock and a dwarf birch-tree formed between them the most luxurious shelter from the noonday sun. Here Bruin had made his lair, and from the tracks on all sides we had no doubt it was one of his favourite summer residences. As he was out, we borrowed his place and had a really good rest there.

In another half-hour we reached the top of the ridge, a series of small peaks with chasms between each, which frustrated our original plan of operations entirely. The summits themselves were covered knee-deep in bilberry bushes, the dark blue fruit of which, where the sun had not yet thawed it, making the most delicious iced dessert I ever tasted.

Looking down on the other side of the ridge, all was ruin and desolation; riven rocks, precipitous walls of grey slate, great fields of moraine, and at the bottom a glacier, from which sprang a considerable stream, whose course eventually led us almost back to camp, but along the most diabolical road any tired sportsman could imagine.

On one of the peaks, in a thin birch-tree, I saw what I am almost certain was a scarlet bullfinch (*Pyrrhula Erythrina*); but if so, the figure in Morris's 'British Birds' is somewhat highly-coloured. It was very tame, and though it saw me, seemed only curious to know who I was, and in no degree suspicious of danger. Whilst I was watching it, hoping to hear its call-note, as some additional clue to its identity, I heard a shrill whistle from the other side the ravine, and there, well out of shot, half-way up an incline accessible only to chamois, flies, members of the Alpine Club, and other creatures with prehensile feet, was a chamois at graze. He had not seen us yet, nor I think got our wind, though the fall of some rocks which we had set in motion during our ascent had startled him from his siesta.

Whilst I was watching him and regretting the impossibility of getting at him, another whistle close to me made me start and grip my rifle nervously. I began to think I must be close to a herd, but peering round an angle of rock, I saw Simon shaping his mouth for a repetition of the call, and so well did he do it, that he brought the suspicious little beast several hundred yards nearer to us, though unfortunately in such a direction that he got our wind, after which his doubts and himself disappeared simultaneously.

On our way back to camp we stirred a troop of four more chamois, two hinds with their fawns, but I was not keen to shoot them, and probably could not have got to them had I been so inclined. Some distance below the glacier, among the river boulders, I saw a specimen of what I should most assuredly have put down as the great copper butterfly, only that I cannot conceive what a great copper was doing in such an unlikely place.

We also saw a bird which I have seen once or twice since in Svânetia, and have not been able to identify. His size was about that of a jay, and his flight somewhat like that bird's, only more undulating and not so clumsy. His head, neck, and shoulders were grey, body apparently chocolate-coloured, while as he flew a crescent of rosy crimson seemed to stretch from wing to wing. A few of the wing feathers appeared to be tipped with white. On the top of the ridge, besides the bullfinch, I saw a pair of finches of some kind, and numerous traces of the presence of what, from Simon's description, I suppose to have been black game; but with the exception of these and a hoopoe or two in the valley by our camp, a landrail flushed in the corn by

Frank, and a black woodpecker or two, Shukachâlo was very destitute of birds.

Frank, it seems, had very soon had enough of the pleasures of mountaineering; in fact, that hatred for all high places which afterwards became a passion with him, had already taken root. After a comfortable snooze on a couch of mountain moss, he had come back early, and set to work like a man at constructing our camp; and a tent firmly erected, and well lined with fern and dry leaves, a blazing fire, something to eat, and a pile of fuel cut into lengths, all ready for burning, bore witness to his energy.

As the corn-fields were close at hand, we did not hurry over our evening meal, but rested and refreshed ourselves at leisure. This Shukachâlo week was certainly the most luxurious time we spent in the Caucasus, and if I wanted to make a good bag of bears and chamois comfortably, Shukachâlo would be one of the first places I should visit.

Having lighted our pipes, Frank and I strolled off, each to his ground, for the night. The big stretch of corn-fields, as being nearer and of greater extent, was assigned to my friend, who, as he had never killed a bear, was the more anxious to do so now.

For me, Simon had decided on a little patch of his own, somewhat higher up the mountain-side, and a good deal further from camp. Here he and I arrived just after sunset, and hid ourselves away behind a fallen tree in the midst of the standing corn.

The evening was perfect. No breath of wind stirred the full ears, not a rustle came from the regiments of dark trees that seemed in the gloaming to be marching down into the little yellow basin of corn-field.

Looking out across the lower end of the basin, we had a view of the course of the now insignificant Rion, as it wound its way far below amongst an endless succession of hills.

Right in front of us, but far away, rose three majestic peaks, between two of which the frozen waves of a great glacier showed from time to time through a kind of foamy rose-coloured mist, half sunset, half coming storm, such as you see so often in Ivazovsky's pictures.

A flight of chattering martins wheeled and manœuvred in the sky, their notes the only ones which broke the perfect stillness. Little by little the rosy light died out, the martins disappeared, the mist cleared off, the trees stood out in darker outline, and the silence became more intense. The stumps of trees in the field seemed to shift and change places in a noiseless, mysterious way, which eluded your sight and hearing equally. Looking along the barrels of my rifle, I became conscious that the foresight, and indeed the end of my barrels was no longer visible. Taking out a piece of white paper, I rolled it round a bit of twine and then fastened it, a clumsy but effective sight, near the muzzle of my rifle.

After waiting another half-hour, Simon's patience became exhausted, and rising he signed to me that it was no good waiting any longer that night. Rather disappointed, I followed him across the field, when just as we were leaving it the sharp, distinct snap of a bough in the forest at our backs set my heart beating. Boughs don't break in that way by themselves, and it was not very long before Simon and I, kneeling, with straining ears, amongst the barley, heard another twig snap, this time just on the confines of the field itself. Then there was absolute silence for ten minutes, and we feared he had winded us and gone, when about two hundred yards below us, moving slowly and silent as a shadow, we made out a great brown form, looking twice its real size in the dim light.

There is something undeniably eery about Bruin at night. The mysterious way in which he appears from the dark recesses of the thick woods or the distant peaks, where he has been keeping out of sight all day; his slow, solemn movements, and the absolute silence he keeps, make him different from all other beasts. The boar can't help grunting out his pleasure, or holding converse with his kind; the wolf and jackal make the night hideous with their howlings; everything else is more or less noisy, but Bruin alone steps out of the darkness, silent as a shadow, to return as noiselessly as he came.

Just below us was a slope of short grass between the patches of standing corn, and here the bear seemed likely to cross. This would be our chance, as the dark line of his back just above the ears of corn did not present the best of marks. Quiet as the big shadow seemed, his progress was scarcely more noiseless than ours, so that when he emerged on one side of the bare patch Simon and I were not a hundred yards from him. As he passed us without a suspicion of our presence, I made a sign to Simon to stand up; and if poor old Michael had looked straight at us the next moment, so blind is he at night, he would probably not have known those two tall dark shapes from the trees around.

Another half-dozen paces into the open, and then as the rifle I am resting on Simon's shoulder rings out on the stillness, the big shadow writhes for a moment on the ground, and then tearing at the wound lurches heavily away into the dark fringe of woods to our right, grunting and groaning horribly as he goes.

The bear never knew where the bullet

came from, and if he had noticed us would probably not have charged; but still Simon was right in refusing to follow him until morning, when I felt pretty confident we should find him.

Whilst we were talking over the events of the last few minutes, one of the big tree-stumps which I had been watching half unconsciously galloped off to another part of the field. Simon saw it as soon as I did, and stalking silently round the lower edge of the basin, we almost ran up against a third bear, when unluckily I coughed, and sent him off in double quick time before I could get a shot at him.

The moonlight was now very brilliant, and the little field seemed literally alive with bears. We distinctly made out four, besides the one I had shot at, and one of them, a very large fellow, with a coat that looked like silver in the moonlight, gave us employment for the next half hour. I could certainly have bagged this bear, but for my guide's intense desire to kill him himself; and as I always find it best to humour these fellows, I let him try to get a shot. Half a dozen times he got fairly near to the stupid brute, but it took such a long time to fix the alpenstock in the ground, and adjust the rifle on the rest so made, that the bear began to move again before my man could pull trigger; and it is an article of the faith of these primitive sportsmen never to waste a charge on a moving object.

At last the bear heard us, and took himself off, when, as the others we had seen were no longer visible, we went back to camp. Here, when my story had been told, an immense amount of hand-shaking had to be gone through with the men, who all looked on my bear as already skinned and brought in. I can't say I felt as comfortable about him, and as it was our first head of big game since we had been in the country, Frank was as keen about it as myself.

The result was that our men were roused uncommonly early next morning, and after a very hurried and slightly indigestible breakfast of skimmed milk, cheese, hazel nuts, and tobacco smoke, we went to look for Bruin.

There we found him, gashed and gory, not a hundred and fifty yards from where he fell, dead and stiff, having apparently had only just strength enough to get back to covert before he died. He was rather a large bear, and we rejoiced over him accordingly; nor was this the first time he had come in contact with man, as a small native bullet which we found just under the skin of his neck clearly proved.

Having skinned him, we left him where he lay, and went back to camp, determined to do no more until evening. As we left the scene of my last night's adventure, we met three young women—friends, relatives, or lovers of Simon's—who were the first of the returning harvesters. They had been here some time already; and had, before commencing work, been collecting a large cloth full of fungi, of a kind which grows on fallen timber. These we bought, and afterwards made into soup.

At the camp a herd of goats just arrived, *en route* to some mountain pastures further up stream, caught the eye of our chief of commissariat; and, in spite of his ignorance of the language, it was not long before Frank had selected a plump little black sheep from among the goats, and was making signs to Simon that he wanted it converted into chops in the shortest possible space of time. Here some religious scruples interfered, and it was not until he had said a very long prayer over his victim, that our man turned butcher.

Whilst this was going on, a very ragged small boy, sole guardian of about forty goats, came down from the grass slopes of the opposite ridge with a batter pudding in a wooden bowl for us, and a present of sour milk. We gave the wee chappie some small silver, whereupon he kissed our hands and went off happy.

All day long Vassili kept croaking about the weather. A snake, he said, had bitten the moon last night, which accounted for its having turned blood red before it set, and presaged bad weather to come. And Vassili was right. As the evening came on, heavy clouds came up all round, and the muttering of the thunder could be heard every now and again amongst the peaks. But fine or stormy, this was the last night on which the fields would be fairly quiet, so Frank and I each moved off to a fresh hunting ground at an early hour, having a somewhat longer trudge than usual to our posts.

The scene of this night's vigil, as far as I was concerned, was between two tiny fields at a great height, divided from one another by a steep grass-bank, so that they looked like two steps of corn. There was a deserted log-hut in one—the lower one, and the forest was so thick on all sides that the place was almost dark before sunset. There were no signs of bear, moreover, so I had very little hope of success; and sat on the grass-bank watching the lower step, while Simon, perched a foot or two above me, watched the upper, listening rather for the hoped-for report of Frank's rifle than for the tread of game coming my way.

Presently the thunderstorm gathered, black and furious, right over our heads, and for a time the big pelting drops drove us into the log-hut for shelter. Presently the rain ceased, and Simon and myself took our places on the slope again, chiefly interested in watching the lightning play among the mountains round us.

Below our place of vantage was a piece of level grass, with here and there a great grey stone upon it. My eyes were unconsciously bent on this spot when a vivid flash of sheet lightning lit up the whole scene, and showed me that what I had only taken for a bigger boulder than the rest was a bear coming slowly and deliberately straight to my feet. Of course I fired as quickly as I could, for he was already within thirty paces, and in another moment would probably have discovered us and bolted. As it was he came down all in a heap, and then picking himself up, plunged forward in our direction. I thought for a moment he was charging, and though I could only see very indistinctly, gave him my second barrel, which missed him clean, but had the effect of turning him.

I have no doubt the idea of attacking us

never entered his head, and his apparent charge was owing to a blind desire to escape from a danger coming from he knew not whence. Be that as it may, he very soon disappeared in the darkness in the direction of our homeward road. This was unlucky, as Simon had a distinct objection to meeting a wounded bear in the dark, and it was now rapidly becoming so dark that we could scarcely find a way through the branches heavy with the drops of the thunder-shower. I don't think I felt quite easy in my mind, as the lightning had become so close and was so vivid that we felt it safer to cover up our guns; and what with this, the darkness, and the denseness of the jungle, it was just as well we did not blunder into the arms of the wounded savage. But we might have spared ourselves our anxiety, for when we went to seek him next morning we found we must have almost walked over his dead body the night before, his strength having scarcely availed him to get clear of the cornfield.

In camp my friend was congratulating himself that our good little tent kept out the heavy rain, and the men were building themselves an awning of boughs, over which they spread the skin of the first bear, after which, having appropriated Frank's bourka, they stretched it over four of them, and so smoking and chatting set the storm at defiance.

With our tea to-night we had an unusual luxury, thanks to the foal we brought with us having decamped; for whatever mare's milk may be like neat, I can vouch for it that the produce of our old mare was a distinct improvement to the tea, and henceforth to milk her was one of our daily duties.

When he had seen us made comfortable for the night, the gallant Simon borrowed my revolver and went off to his lower corn-field to protect his three lady friends. Shortly afterwards, Vassili went too, and the rascals were not worth their salt for a couple of days afterwards. Such is the effect of love. On their way up they met a bear at rather close quarters, but being only armed with my revolver, they wisely let him alone.

There is little doubt in my mind that in spite of the reapers we should have got more bears had we stayed on at Shukachâlo, but as he had not been lucky, Frank was tired of the place; and for my part, having killed a good many bears before, I was more anxious to get on into Svânetia for mountain game, than to stay on here, however successfully. So on September 1 we hauled down our tent, and packing it and our trophies on the old mare, marched up stream for the much talked of pastures of Lapûr.

Before I close this chapter, let me say to any one who cares to kill bears and chamois, I know no better centre than the old town of Gebi. From there you can go to Shukachálo before harvest, or during the feast at the end of August, and I am convinced that at least one day out of every three you ought to bag either chamois or bear, while you can always get provisions sent from Gebi to your camp. But for bears, if a large bag of these beasts is your object, you should go in June, when the snow is only just leaving the hillsides, when there are no fruits and no crops, and the only food is the young grass, as it springs green and tender where the sun has melted away the snow.

Here, so say the natives, in the spring (*i.e.* end of May and June) you may see parties of bears, from two or three to six or eight in number, gaunt with their long winter's fast, and with their coats rough and thin. Whether they would be worth shooting in this condition I don't know; but as a matter of experience, if it were not for his surroundings, the shooting of a bear is not productive of much excitement. Perhaps when they were hungry and in company they might make things a trifle too exciting; but of this I cannot speak, as I never tried it, and the natives I have come across are in the same position.

CHAPTER VI.

BY THE SOURCE OF THE RION.

'TWENTY miles at least from Shukachálo to Lapûr.' Such was the verdict of our guides, but knowing how little idea they had of distance we rather doubted their statement. At about 8 A.M. we started, determined to do the distance in one day, a feat which our men declared impossible. For once they were nearly right; it was a really hard day's work, almost too hard for the old mare and for my friend's heart. It was not until after those weary hills that he began to suspect that mountaineering made his heart beat a trifle faster than it had any right to, and when I put my hand on it and felt it thumping against his sides, I was fairly frightened, though I admired his pluck for doing the heavy collar work we had been doing all day as gamely as he had done.

The first few versts were easy going enough, the track being by the bed of the Rion, with our faces set towards the peak and glacier of Erden. As we crossed the Kalmac, a small tributary of the Rion, I actually saw and caught a tiny trout, just enough for me to be able to swear that there are such fish in these streams.

By the banks of the Rion, we noticed for the first time to-day the lovely velvety wings of the Camberwell beauty, a butterfly that during the rest of my journey became the very commonest of all the many objects of beauty around us. Near villages they seemed as difficult to catch as they would be in England, but about Lapûr they were as tame as domestic creatures, settling close to and on more than one occasion absolutely upon my person. Is it I wonder a matter of common knowledge that butterflies are like birds and other living things, in that, where they know man they avoid him, but where he is new to them, are as fearless as birds under similar circumstances?

Towards ten o'clock we left the river-bed, and then it was that our work began; and remembering that to-day was September 1, thoughts crossed our mind of those cool places under high hawthorn hedges in Old England where, when the morning's ground had been beaten, the hamper would be unpacked, and certain sparkling 'refreshers' from bottles brilliant in silver foil, or big-bellied honest brown jugs, would be administered to the weary gunner. Alas, that we had nothing better to drink your health in 'St. Partridge' than the mountain stream afforded: none of your devotees would have pledged you in a deeper draught than Frank and I as we toiled up those endless grass slopes.

At first we faced the long slope of green hills gaily enough—it would be a good climb, but we could see the end of it; and even when we had gained a view of another equally high beyond it we did not despair. But when four o'clock came and hill after hill, each longer than the other, rolled endlessly upwards from every ridge we gained, I joined heartily with Frank in anathematising such a lying landscape, and devoutly agreed with him that this sort of scenery would be greatly improved by being rolled out flat.

On the very top—for we did get there eventually, and found it to be between four and five thousand feet above sea level—we found still traces of the wandering tribe of Bruin, though whether he had come there to enjoy the view or grub up the roots of the few canary coloured crocuses which grew there remained a mystery.

Below us lay ranges of low rocky hills, covered with rhododendron scrub and a scattered wood of birches. Two or three small rivers met in the valleys below, and opposite to our great grass fells were the glaciers and peaks of Lapûr, Yedenna, and Passimta, whence issues the infant Rion.

In the valley at the foot of Lapûr we pitched our tent and listened to Simon's account of the wild doings of Svânetians and the men of Radcha on this border-land ten years ago. Even now the capital goat pastures and sheep runs of Lapûr are seldom used, for over the glacier of Matchkapar is a pathway risky to cross and uninviting to look at, over which even in the present days of peace the roving men of Svânetia and the Tartars from the other side the range not unfrequently steal down upon the unsuspecting shepherds of Gebi.

In spite of the good day's work we had done Simon and I, for the larder's sake, made a short investigation of the nearer hillsides, hoping to add a chamois steak to the humble meal of maize bread and water with which we must otherwise end the day. Meanwhile, Frank pitched the tent, so that when we came in empty-handed at dusk we had at least somewhere to lay our heads.

When limbs are fairly tired, and the digestion not tasked beyond its powers, the nights seem shorter by half than they are at home in England, and it seemed to me that I had only just dozed off with my pipe between my teeth when Simon shook me up to say a chamois was in sight. 'Hang the chamois!' was certainly my first remark, or something at least as strong; and when in a generous mood I offered the shot to Frank, rousing him to do so, his remarks were made in such extremely graphic Berkshire that I fairly fled. Never did mortal man feel less inclined for early rising than I did on September 2, and my legs were so stiff from the work of the previous day that I could almost fancy I heard them creak as I bent them.

After an hour's climb, we were lying on a knoll above the dell wherein the chamois was feeding, waiting until the old buck should have finished his breakfast and composed himself for his morning nap. He looked a splendid beast as the light fell on his redbrown sides, wet with the dew he brushed off the tangle of larkspur, through beds of which, bright with its blue blossoms, he had made his way to the wild thyme on which he was then feeding.

Unluckily, when the sun began to dry up the dew and make the place too warm for our chamois, he moved off at a dainty trot to a thicket of birch trees, and here probably lay down for the day. We never saw him again at any rate that day.

The next three days of our stay at Lapûr were days of fasting and bad luck. When we got back to camp after our early morning stalk, we found the last scrap of meat was finished, and our morning meal had to be one of maize cakes and currants, a pretty sounding *menu*, but one which does little towards filling the aching void.

As the sun got stronger, a plague of flies manifested itself, small stupid beasts, who had not the least idea of avoiding the hand of the avenger, but generally managed to extract a drop of your blood before vengeance overtook them.

Naturally our thoughts reverted to our pipes, and having filled and lighted them, our enemies fled for a time. 'By the way, old fellow,' said Frank, 'that's the last pipe of my bird's-eye, I suppose we shall have to take to the beastly cigarette tobacco those fellows smoke.'

For some weeks past my friend, with a good nature none but smokers can appreciate, had provided me with tobacco, a supply of the soothing weed being the one thing I had forgotten on leaving home. Now even his monster pouch was empty, and on inquiry we were horrified to hear that Platon, our interpreter, had given the last of our stock of native tobacco to the priest at Gebi. So for days there was neither meat nor tobacco in the camp. We had a little tea left, which we used to drink out of a couple of wooden bowls; but as our sugar was all finished and it took some time to get used to the salt which the men substituted for it, to say nothing of the fine woody flavour which the tea drew from our cups, even tea drinking was not an unmixed pleasure.

As for the men, the tobacco famine fell on

their spirits with a crushing effect; life without a pipe was a thing unbearable, so before long I noticed old Vassili come to the fireside with some dried leaves of a big hollow-stemmed plant (*Angelica officinalis*), which grew in quantities all over the hillside. This he chopped very fine, and by dint of holding a live coal to the pipe during the whole operation, got a smoke out of it. Simon seemed to prefer the pith of what I fancy was a kind of willow, smoking it in its stem, cigar fashion. These substitutes, however well they might suit the men, were more than our heads could stand, though we subsequently managed to extract some grains of consolation from a pipe filled with the scrapings off the outside of a burnt maize cake.

Fruit was our one luxury, and I know of nothing more refreshing than the huge pear-shaped purple currants, which grew in quantities all round us. This fruit is not altogether like any I have seen elsewhere, the shape being different, the berry larger; and though the colours vary from that of our red to our black currant, the fruit, even when withering, never tastes quite ripe. Once we tried a fruit pudding, being anxious to demonstrate to our natives their folly in never using the fruits round them for cooking purposes.

Except in its raw state the Svânetians and men of Radcha make no use whatever of the vast quantities of fruit which ripen and fall unused on every hillside in their country. Fond as he is of it, there is such a prodigal supply of raspberries and currants that even Bruin is dainty, picking and choosing as he feeds.

Unfortunately our efforts at reform in this matter were not as successful as they deserved to be. Neither Frank nor I knew the secret of making a crust, moreover, we had no sugar; and in the end the huge mess of bluish porridge which we produced, served only to stamp more decidedly our friend Deto as a man of appetite invincible. Even he, though he shovelled it down manfully, remarked from time to time that he thought it would have been very good without the currants.

Meanwhile, where was Platon? Day after day we scanned the crest of the ridge above us, but no vision of a dirty white tcherkesska rewarded our investigations. Had he indeed gone off smiling with our thirty pounds in his pocket, and should we never see his hungry-looking face again? It began to look extremely probable.

We had rigged up our tent on the piece of ground most nearly level within reach of our camp, and though that was on such a slope that Frank, who had taken the lower side, had to be kept in by a kind of earth-work, so great was his power of sleeping that he got through the night very comfortably.

As for me, I was grieved more than I cared to tell him, to notice how the want of food was telling on his manly form, the fact being that when in my sleep I began to roll down on top of him his elbows and ribs seemed to have acquired a power of penetration not natural to them under happier circumstances.

We had one great luxury at Lapûr. Coming down from the birch wood was a stream of the clearest, coldest water that any tub-loving Briton ever revelled in. Just before getting into the valley, some huge boulders had dammed its course, forming a natural bath-room with a continual supply of fresh water, and natural curtains of ferns and currant bushes. Here we passed some of our happiest moments, though here also was laid upon us that last straw which nearly broke the back of our endurance.

There is a beast, a creeping thing, which many worthy Mussulmen seem to love to rear upon their persons. To the improperly educated Englishman the mere mention of this creature is an offence. Judge then of our consternation when we found that we too were not exempt from the wandering hordes of this insect pest.

Quick as we could get them off, shirt followed jersey and coat waistcoat into the depths of our bathing pool, and here with boulders piled upon them we left them, walking back to camp in naked innocence. For the rest of that day we devoted ourselves to the laundry, and during the whole of our stay at Lapûr always had one shirt on, and another in the wash-tub.

Every night before turning in to rest, our men insisted on our loading our weapons, as they suffered from a lively fear of wandering Svânetians. Three of these gentry passed us without a word the day after we arrived; wild-looking fellows with long, unkempt hair, and dressed entirely in sheepskins, driving the most miserably thin cow human eyes ever gazed on. They had come down the glacier, so that for some time it would be useless to watch for tûr at their drinking place, as these shy beasts would leave the peak for a day or two after having seen men upon it.

Every day Frank and myself went out in search of game, he generally taking the river bed, whilst I climbed to the top of the ridge. Twice I saw chamois, and once, after watching the pretty beasts' camp in a position which we thought accessible, Vassili and I essayed to stalk them. What a subject they would have made for such a pencil as Wolfe's, as they lay grouped round a rocky knoll, on the very summit of which, in the shadow of a thin birch bush, lay the leader of the herd!

After a long and difficult stalk, as we crept down a steep incline above them, up went Vassili's heels, and with a crash he shot through a bed of dry rhododendrons, almost into the middle of them. Most of the chamois had disappeared at the first sound of his sudden descent; but when Vassili managed to stop himself, there was one small head looking about in a puzzled way over the top of a heap of boulders about one hundred yards below.

Vassili made signs to me, and as quickly as I could I got to his side; but long before I could get to him, my worthy hunter had erected his alpenstock, rested his rifle thereon and—frightened away my last chance. I refrained from kicking Vassili, and was rewarded by getting a long shot at two of the herd as they scampered up the opposite side of the ravine. One of these I believe I hit very hard, but though we marked the place into which it seemed to fall, we could never find it.

So we went home again to the tune of 'Ararrees' (pigeon Georgian for 'haven't got anything!'). This continued want of food and success was now really beginning to tell on us, as indeed a life sustained on currants and hope very well might; and on Saturday morning, as Platon had not re-appeared, we determined to send out Deto, the cook, on a foraging expedition.

Simon had an idea that there was somewhere on the Radcha side of the hills a herd of goats feeding, which had left Gebi as soon as the shepherds had heard that there would be a chance of pasturing their beasts on the slopes of Lapûr, under the protection of the redoubted Simon and the rifles of the Englishmen with him.

It was past the hour of dusk that evening, and we had been forced to sup as usual on maize gruel, when the sight of Deto and the old mare toiling down the hillside roused fresh hopes and appetites within us. On his saddle he had a small black sheep, still alive, bound in such brutal fashion that the cords had cut through its skin, and must have caused it exquisite torture. In spite of his success in the foraging line, Deto got into very hot water that night, and if he ever fetches a sheep for another Englishman he will probably kill the poor brute before tying it on to his saddle.

Once the *coup de grâce* had been administered by Simon, it was wonderful to see the way in which that sheep changed in appearance. In about an hour the only trace left of it was its curly black coat, and a single leg of mutton hanging to a pole by the fireside, all the rest of the carcase being either devoured or cooking in our caldron.

All that night Simon, Vassili, and Deto never left off eating. Deto especially had barely time to speak, so busy was he making maize cakes and eating entrails, which he dug from time to time out of the embers with his fingers. Though no men can stand starvation better than these Caucasian mountaineers, Simon being especially gifted in that way, once let them get hold of meat and they gorge with the same greediness and improvidence that disgusts one in the African savage. Looking at Deto, our cook, by the firelight, one knew what the face of a were wolf should be like.

On Sunday evening our larder was nearly as bare as before Deto's expedition, and it did not want this last inducement to action to make me determine that I would do all I knew in the next few days to change my luck.

Nearly three weeks had gone by, and although I had killed a couple of bears, I had not yet secured a single head of chamois or ibex. At dusk on Sunday I lay down for a few hours, after which my men roused me in the dark, and all unwilling, with misty eyes and uncertain steps, I had to follow my swift, silent Simon over unseen boulders, which threatened dislocation at every blind stride, through tall tangled weeds, heavy and wet with the night dew, drenching and chilling us to the bone, through groves of willows which swung back viciously as Simon passed, and cut his follower sharply across the face.

Once out of the thickets of the low land, we had a stiff up-hill scramble for half an hour, then we plunged waist-deep through a stream that came down from the glacier, close to the foot of which we now were, ten more minutes along a narrow break-neck ledge covered with short dry mountain grass, the last half-dozen steps so ticklish that I was not ashamed to grip Simon's helping hand, and then swing round a sharp projecting corner into a little straw-lined cave, which was our post for the night.

A rumour had reached us that a party of hunters from Svânetia had been about the glacier for some days past, and as Simon thought it quite possible they might dispute our possession of the eyrie, he had insisted on Frank and Vassili joining our party. When, however, we found no trace of any rivals, he listened to Frank's suggestion, and the end of it was that my friend and his hunter went back to camp.

How it was that in these mountaineering exploits we never suffered from cold and rheumatism, or any of the other ills that assail us at home, I could never quite comprehend. All that night, for example, I passed shivering on my rocky ledge, wet to my waist and chilled by the wind that whistled over the glacier. But I never felt any evil results from the exposure next day.

As soon as the moon rose, we kept a very careful outlook, but of course the wind shifted, and when next morning we began with stiff limbs the climb to the top of the glacier, which we had determined on the night before, we found that the 'djikve' had come to within about a hundred yards of the spot at which they would have been within sight and range of our rifles, and then, getting our wind, turned and bolted.

During our night watch, the peaks above had been to us as another world, still with an awful silence, cloud-wrapped and full of mystery, from which we waited for the wily mountain beasts to creep down to our world below. Now, as we faced their stiff ascents, they were revealed to us in all their wild barrenness. Of herbage there seemed absolutely none, but ridge upon ridge of hard argillaceous rock, its inverted strata brittle as glass, but with edges sharp as razors lacerated our feet and hands until my mocassins were red with my own blood.

The only flower we saw was a large kind of daisy with a yellow centre, surrounded by a circle of close pink petals.

Twice we caught vanishing glimpses of

chamois, but on both occasions well out of range. Wherever we climbed the rocks were covered with the droppings of chamois and ibex, and we constantly heard the long whistle and saw the strong grouse-like flight of those splendid birds, the Caucasian snow partridges (*Tetrao Caucasicus*), which abound throughout the peaks round Lapûr, and in all the mountain range of Svânetia and Daghestan. Wherever the mountains are most bleak, destitute of all herbage, and the crumbling slopes are most patched with snow, the long wild whistle of these birds used to attract our attention. Their colour makes them hard to distinguish amongst the grey rocks which form their home, and even when you have seen them alight it is by no means easy to keep your eye on them, as they run and crouch like French partridges amongst the stones.

Once I came upon an old cock going

through a sort of war dance by himself on a terribly dizzy place, and watched him with his tail spread like a turkey's over his back, sidling and curtseying for a long time, but it was not until I threw a stone at his head that I knew the hens were running about near him. I had a great mind to shoot him for some of my naturalist friends in England, even though it cost me all chance of a chamois or ibex for the day; but I reflected on the state he would be in after coming in contact with an 'Express' bullet, and spared him.

Frank tried once or twice to secure some of these birds, but cruel fate, which was always throwing them in the way of my rifle, never gave him a chance with his No. 12. As a rule, I fancy he was hardly high enough for them; for these birds live in exactly the same places as the ibex, and where you find one the other will not be far distant.

It was broad daylight when we at last

emerged on a moraine not far from the summit; and running across it, cut the path over the glacier from the Tartar country on the other side. That it was not too safe a road, the remains of a man and the bleached bones and broken saddle-trees of his two horses scattered broadcast amongst snow and rocky débris, bore painful testimony. Poor fellow! he must have been a Tartar I should think of the richer classes, as the paper of his tobacco which we found showed it to be of an expensive manufactured brand, and not the rough native stuff smoked by the men of Radcha.

The greater part of the day was spent by us wandering about along the ruinous paths of former avalanches, among the highest of the sterile snow-covered peaks, and in all places where that wildest of earth's denizens, the Caucasian ibex, was likely to be found; but, alas! for our evil fate, other sportsmen had been before us, and our prey had moved off to lonelier fastnesses.

Not once or twice but many times during the day, we came across the lairs of Svânetian hunters; dens like the dens of wild beasts, between great masses of upright slate rock, on the very edge of the highest ridges.

What always seemed most strange to me in the nature of these men, when I came to know them afterwards, was that there seemed so little superstition or poetry amongst them. Surely some wild legends should grow out of the minds of men who pass long solitary nights in these lonely heights, their only music the keen shrill signal of the chamois or 'djikve,' the rush of the wild hawk's wing, as it brushes close past their lair, the throbbing of the mountain breezes round the peaks, and the murmur of the mountain stream. But if they had any folk lore amongst them, if the armies of mist and cloud and the voices of Nature in her loneliest moods, had any subtle signification for them, my interpreter never had tact enough to draw them out, and ignorance of their language prevented me using my opportunities.

Neither did I ever meet in the Caucasus with that 'habitual melancholy of the mountaineer' of which I have read once or twice ; faces full of sad resignation to their lives of hardship, drawn and earnest with frequent looking on death. *Au contraire*, my mountaineers as a rule were hard, energetic fellows, with faces tanned by wind and rain, bright and ruddy with frequent baths of pure mountain air, but by the camp fire garrulous fellows, with the spirits and appetites of men in hard training, and a power of smoking bad tobacco whilst climbing the longest and stiffest ascents, which must be witnessed to be believed However, the mists were gathering, so casting a last glance over the ridge towards Kabardah and the land of the Tscherk Tartars, lands which I mentally determined to explore another day, we scrambled back to camp.

I don't think that night either Frank or I said much ; we were both hungry, and one at any rate dead beat. But there was to be no rest for me. Long before the dawn had really come, Vassili and Simon had me out of my bourka, and told me we must start at once for another peak to our rear, called Luxhánova. I felt as if I could not possibly do another hard day's work yet, and turned wistful eyes on Frank ; but a better mood prevailed, and I remembered that I had not two more months in the Caucasus, and there would be lots of time for sleep and no chance of ibex in England. So I hastily made up a cast of flies for my chum, who was in my absence to have a try for trout in a neighbouring stream, the Khedovra, and then followed my men up the sloping fells.

No one spoke for the first hour or so ; the men were smoking and plodding steadily upwards, one just above me, the other below. It was early morning when we got to the top of the **fells** above our camp, and along the edges **of** the precipices on the other side several coveys of snow partridges were whistling lustily.

For another hour we kept along the top of the fells, and then we branched off on to a spur of mountains which led to and terminated in the peak and district of **Lukhan.** Good heavens! what liars those Lukhan peaks are! Every slope along whose narrow edge we toiled painfully upwards promised to be the **last,** but were we ever so strong, ever so patient, were the peak ever so high, another peak higher more wearisome was always ready to rise with painful regularity to replace the one we had just topped.

About noon we sat down and ate **a** maize

cake apiece, scraping off some of its outer crust to provide us with a pipe after lunch; we drank and laved our hands and feet and faces at a little stream which welled from an ice field in the saddle between two neighbouring peaks, and then we gripped our alpenstocks and plodded on.

So sharp were the upturned edges of the rocks that my sandals were hardly sound enough to hold the mountain grass we put into them, and before night my bleeding feet were absolutely bare. The men were in just as bad a plight, or the good fellows would have given me their sandals and gone barefoot themselves.

About three o'clock I suppose it was when we got to the downs of Luxhan, splendid little tablelands of short grass between high glacier-adorned peaks on all sides. Here we sat and rested for a few minutes, and here too lost the track of a huge old bear, who seemed to have preceded us the whole of our journey until now. But here, alas! we found a track far more formidable to us than that of the bear. There it was, plain enough, the impress of a sandal, and the square little hole in which the wearer of it had stuck his mountaineer's pike. What with the fatigue and the disappointment of again finding someone before me, in a place not known to one hunter in ten among the neighbouring villages, I fairly lost heart, and I could hardly believe my ears when Simon crept to my side and whispered 'Djikve arrees' (there's an ibex).

The tableland of grass on which we were ended abruptly in a precipice, from which we looked down on a glacier, several hundred feet below. On the opposite side the glacier rose a bare precipitous wall of rock, reaching far above the level of the tableland on which we stood, to the topmost crags of Luxhan. On this wall, which as the crow flies was not so very far from us, on about the same level as ourselves, Simon's keen eyes had made out an ibex. At first sight and at the distance I might have mistaken it for a chamois, but bringing the glass to bear, I made out a grand ram, with broad sweeping horns, standing on the narrowest of ledges, utterly unsuspicious of our presence, entirely taken up with the 'lick' of bitter water at which it was refreshing itself.

We had lots of time to look about us, but look as we would there was no possibility of stalking the ibex, in fact no way of approaching a yard nearer than we now were. Had we had Frank's long range rifle with us we might have had a chance. As it was I could hope for nothing but failure with my 'Express.' But it was the only thing to do, so allowing for the distance as well as I could I fired. My men had focussed the animal with their glasses, and a simultaneous exclamation of surprise came from each of them. Dear me! how well my wild goat chase might have a successful end here if only I could say that bullet struck three inches lower. Unluckily it did not, and the beast, tossing its head in surprise, trotted a few yards along the ledge and stood at gaze.

Again I fired, this time getting even closer than before, so said my men, but still the beast was untouched; and now, thoroughly roused to the danger of his position, was going wildly straight up the wall-like face of the cliff. So steep was the road he chose that from where we were, we had the same view of his back that you have of a fly's as he crawls up the window pane. I sent two more bullets after him, in the vain hope of a lucky shot securing for me the coveted head even now; but though one fell so near him as almost to frighten him into a false step, he got away untouched. I had still four cartridges left and some two or three hours of daylight, so my men and myself climbed down to the glacier, and tried to find a way to the crags from which our escaped prey had descended.

It was getting late when we found a feasible path, and my men begged me to stay where we were for the night, as there was wood and water, and a place which some hunter had used before as a camp. But I am ashamed to say I had lost my temper, and nothing would do for me but another effort among the peaks while daylight lasted. My men's remonstrances fell unheeded, or only met with a good rating in return; and it speaks well for them that they followed me in spite of my folly, until that happened which they had predicted.

Having climbed about half way to the point at which we hoped to find ibex, and being well out of range of wood and water, the mists and the darkness came down upon us, making further progress impossible, so that the best we could do was to select the biggest boulder near us, and arranging our one bourka so as to afford as much shelter as possible to all three, we curled ourselves up and waited for morning.

I have had some rough nights in my life; one on a high peak in Daghestan on Christmas Eve, and another carrying reindeer we had killed over the heavy going of a valley in Spitzbergen to our boat, but for genuine misery I don't think any ever beat that night at Luxhan. In Daghestan I think we had tobacco, and I know we had high hopes for the morrow; while, in spite of the thirstiness of a long-legged Scotchman I had with me, there was beer in that boat in Spitzbergen; but here, on this hillside at Luxhan, it was bitterly cold and damp: we had no fire, no water (had had none either since noon), and only one pipe of bread crumbs between three. When that pipe was out the men rewarded me for sharing it with them by giving me the inner corner under the boulder, and then lying on top of me to keep me warm.

I don't fancy any of my friends in England would care about Simon and Vassili's ragged persons for bedfellows, but a man perishing with cold on a damp hillside gets over a great deal of squeamishness in a night, and I was heartily thankful to put up with my ragged companions for the warmth they gave me.

In the morning we could see water about two hours' march below us, and the way to it was the straight road into Svânetia, *viâ* Lascheti. I felt almost inclined to adopt it and send back for the rest of my party rather than face the *viâ diabolica* home to Lapûr. But eventually the road to Lapûr was the road we took, and I would rather think of the moment when I lay down with my mouth to a stream of snow water at 1 P.M. than of

BRIDGE OF KIDESDALE.

the weary hours I passed plodding up to it with bleeding feet during the most tiring morning I remember.

I was done to a turn, and I remember counting my steps on the way home, and wondering how many hundreds I should have to count before arriving at the top of each ascent. I know that whenever I raised my eyes at the end of say 300 or 1,000 I invariably seemed no nearer than when I began to count. But when our camp came in sight, and Frank, the sybarite, was seen surrounded by visitors, an object of interest (and doubtless of admiration), to a troop of Caucasian shepherds, I almost ran the rest of the way home, despite my bleeding feet.

The long-expected herd had arrived at last. One of its members was already hanging by his heels to the pole of our larder; two bowls of milk had been abstracted by Frank from the mothers of the herd as a fine for butting at and otherwise maltreating our tent ; the shepherds had supplied a stock of coarse tobacco, and though tired and unsuccessful, that Wednesday night was a red letter night in our camp life.

We slept early that night, but Simon and Vassili were getting keen about the reward they had been promised for the first head of mountain game killed, so I was turned out again at 5.30 next morning to face my old enemy, the hill, again. Frank started with me, though in a different direction, in search of snow partridges. Of course he had no luck, while equally of course I saw quantities of birds, one covey of ten, young birds, too, chuckling and clucking on a hillside all round me, like barn-door fowls, for nearly ten minutes.

On our way up to the heights where the djikve live we again sighted the big solitary chamois buck, who had cost me a good deal of climbing once or twice before. This time

I managed the stalk myself; but just at the critical moment, as he was sleeping with one eye open, the old rascal caught sight of Frank and Vassili coming up the hill below him, and he was up and away instantly. In sheer desperation I risked a shot at him, which, though it missed him (he was four hundred yards off at least), turned him down hill. Quick as he was, Simon was hardly less active, and managed to get down to a point several hundred yards below in time to get another shot at him.

Lucky Simon! The chamois gave him a shot at about sixty yards, which he, as usual, missed. But Fortune was kind to-day. Twice headed, the buck now came straight up-hill, evidently determined to make for some of those mountain fastnesses wherein he felt himself safe from the annoyances of mankind. But *en route* he was obliged to pass me. This time he came within about 150 yards, and as he cantered up a watercourse I gave a whistle which for the moment brought him to a standstill. I never could shoot lying down, so jumping up I threw up my rifle as he started off wildly again, and rolled him over with a bullet, well home behind the shoulder.

I have seen a good many heads of chamois killed in the Caucasus since, but none to beat, and very few to equal, that of this my first buck. No doubt if he had not had such large horns or so red a hide, he might have passed for a denizen of greater heights, but I was well content with him as he was, and as I look at his head in my dining-room, I don't in the least regret the weary days he cost me. By comparing my heads with heads of chamois killed in Switzerland, I find the Caucasian much the smaller of the two.

After my four days' hard work, it was a luxury to be back in camp by 9 A.M., let alone the unusual satisfaction of coming back with game; and though my chamois, being an old one, made the least savoury soup imaginable, I had no cause to complain of my game being unappreciated.

In camp I found two of the shepherds looking rather down in the mouth, in consequence of the illness of their third companion. When I passed their camp at dawn this fellow was grovelling on the ground in all the agonies occasioned by a too plentiful repast of unripe fruit. I had, at their request, given him a note to Frank, who it seems had dosed him, to the best of his abilities, with a decoction of laudanum, which we had with us for the cure or prevention of cholera. As Frank had no notion of the dose to be taken, and the man seemed very ill, he (to use his own words) poured him out about half a tablespoonful, 'which, having swallowed, that shepherd naturally slept.' But such was the man's constitution that, though he slept all that day and night, he woke next morning very pale but quite free from his internal pains. Frank was rewarded by local rank of Doctor, and frequent unauthorised supplies of goat's milk.

That night we had a grand dinner, entertaining the shepherds with my old billy goat, while we fed on mutton; and after dinner, having thrown on fresh logs and lighted our pipes, we made a musical night of it—Frank waking the echoes with 'John Peel,' 'The place where the old horse died,' and similar sporting ditties (which, unfortunately, I had to translate), and the men in return crooning some of their native songs.

CHAPTER VII.

LAPÛR TO USHKÛL.

On Friday, September 8, our long-lost interpreter, Platon, was viewed on the top of the fells above us, and so great was our joy that it required a mighty effort to put the proper amount of silent, dignified rebuke into our manner in receiving him. With Platon as guard, guide, and porter, came another brother of Vassili's, a fine-looking fellow, who was at once taken into our service. On going into matters with our truant we found that, though he had been a very expensive messenger, some misdirections of mine were partly to blame for it, and in the end we had obtained what we most wanted—money.

That night we made all our arrangements for a start into Svânetia on the morrow, and were debating on the advisability of having one more vigil at the nest below the glacier, when a huge array of black clouds sweeping up our valley from the south-west settled the question for us. These clouds were the vanguard of winter, and next morning all the higher mountains wore a thin mantle of newly-fallen snow, while in the valleys rain had swollen all the streams, and made our party pass a most unpleasant night.

Our men under their awning covered with my skins slept and would have been fairly happy had not the rain put out their fire; but for Frank and myself, in our ill-arranged little *tente d'abri*, it was absolutely necessary that we should sit upright in constrained positions to prevent our bodies touching the canvas, for whenever that happened in came our enemy the rain. So we sat up all night, consuming no little of Platon's tobacco, while from time to time the vivid sheet-lightning gave us quaint glimpses of the interior of which we were the centre.

Luckily for us, our little tent weathered the storm, and towards morning we got an hour or two for sleep, after which I had to go through the usual difficulties with my men before making a new start. First they did not want to go into Svânetia at all, then they must be prepaid, and as I would not agree to that suicidal arrangement, the money must be paid over to Platon in their presence, to be held for them until the end of their engagement. Then they must go back to Gebi for more provisions, to say good-bye to their wives, to make arrangements for the tending of their cattle, to get more horses, and finally they urged that the country was impracticable for horses, and they must go back for more bearers. But as I made no concessions to them, and they saw no chance of screwing a higher rate of pay out of me, I at last got them under weigh by about eleven.

Our road lay down the banks of the river, which our men called Lapûr, but which I presume is that marked in the Russian map as 'Tsxenis-tsxale,' until its junction with another small stream, which they called Khedowra. Road of course there was none, and so wooded and steep were the banks that we were continually obliged to cross and recross the stream. To keep ourselves dry we accomplished this crossing by leap-frogging on to the quarters of our baggage animals, and stretching over pots, pans, and other impedimenta, clinging frantically to their manes. The position was difficult to maintain, as the horses stumbled about among the boulders of the river bed, and afforded subject for long and hearty laughter.

About two o'clock we reached the junction

of the two streams, near which on the left-hand bank we found the most wonderful fruit forest I ever saw. The whole of the undergrowth for over a couple of miles was almost entirely composed of currant bushes and raspberry canes, principally the latter, and every bough weighed down with fruit. It was hopeless to try to hurry our men through this tract; and, much as I enjoyed the delicious fruit myself, long before I got to my journey's end I would have given a great deal that every fruit tree between Gebi and Djuaria had been barren in the year 1882. We lost half our time whilst the men were gathering fruit by the way.

In the angle formed by the junction of the two streams was the best camping ground we had seen as yet. A large open space, covered with abundance of fine tussocky grass, water on two sides of it, and a semi-circle of beautiful low hills running round it and down into the fruit forest. Here, amongst the raspberry canes, the bears had established regular thoroughfares; and, though I knew well how much 'sign' one bear is capable of leaving behind him, I am quite sure that this corner among the hills must have been the regular habitat of at least a couple of dozen of these animals. Had Frank cared to stay I should have acquiesced in a three or four days' camp here; but as he did not, and bears were not the first object of my travels, we moved on, and I content myself with pointing the spot out to anyone who follows in my steps.

Once or twice during the day we saw chamois, and wasted an hour or two stalking them, gaining nothing thereby but a confirmation of a former impression, that once chamois have sighted you, however favourable the ground, time spent in stalking is time thrown away.

After leaving our noon-day halting-place we turned up a gully to the west, and forced our way painfully through the thickets of weeds and flowers which clothe the foot-hills below the ridge which separates the river Lapûr from the river Zesku. These surmounted, our men began to look serious, and our troubles really commenced. The pass which they intended to cross by was known only to Vassili, and his memory of it was but indistinct, so that before long it became evident that the chances were we should not get over it that night.

For a human being the ascent was steep enough to try every muscle to the utmost, but for horses, and laden horses too, the way seemed impracticable. Still so wonderful are the mountaineering feats performed by these poor-looking screws of the Caucasus that we persevered slowly upwards, and had almost accomplished our task when one of our horses gave in, turned restive, bit and plunged, all but coming over backwards down the narrow way, in doing which he would certainly have carried one or more of us with him. But Simon stuck manfully to his head, and we cleared out from behind him with that speed care for one's personal safety excites in the most weary, and for the moment the catastrophe was averted.

The top of the pass is a narrow saddle with high banks on each side, and so thin is the edge of the ridge here that there is not level standing room for a horse at the top. Here the restive one elected to have another revolt, and succeeded in landing himself on his side, hopelessly cast on the very summit, the chief question in our minds being whether he would slide head first into the valley of the Zesku, or back into the country from which we had come. Meanwhile, such of our property as we did not lay hands on at once went hopping down hill again. By dint of every man doing all he could to help ; by the exertion of immense energy and marvellous strength on Simon's part, we, in the course of an hour, had saved our baggage and piled it in safety, and what was more unhoped for had got the horse on his legs again.

The dusk was now coming on apace, and one glance over the edge at the road before us was enough to convince the most foolhardy that even goats if laden could not hope to accomplish the descent successfully. So after a long palaver Déto, our cook, was paid off, furnished with food, tobacco, and a rifle, and though very frightened and averse to the undertaking, started back to Lapûr in charge of the horses for Gebi. Then each man shouldered all he could carry, and any foolish pride which I had till then entertained in my own strength vanished for ever, as I saw the enormous load which by common consent was awarded to Simon as his share. No Turkish porter of Constantinople, no Swiss mountaineer (not even Adolphe Foliguet, who I remember to have seen carry a heavy English lady from 'les Pendants' to the valley with scarcely a pause to get his wind again) but I venture to assert would have hesitated before he undertook Simon's task that night.

We got safely down the precipitous part of the descent while there was still some light in the sky; but before we had been blundering blindly in the first belt of wood between us and the valley much more than an hour, night set in—a night without a moon, and no stars visible through the clouds. At first the men tried hard to find a way down to the open, but we soon found that the end of this would be a false step over a precipice, or the straying of some member of our party. Then we hoped that in the valley below there might be some Sváns, with their flocks, to whom the hidden ways of the hillsides were known ; but no answer came back to our whistlings and shoutings, so we had to give it up and camp where we were.

The worst part of it was, there was not a place anywhere bare enough of scrub and bramble, all dripping wet, on which to camp, and eventually we heaved our loads into a comparatively low blackberry bush, spread our bourkas over them, and sat down very wet and miserable indeed. In time we managed to make a fire, which only served to show us what a very uncomfortable thicket we were sitting in the middle of, and then having taken a preventative dose of quinine and a pipe, we curled ourselves into our bourkas—cold, thirsty, and sulky.

I believe, in the night, unlike Dr. Watts's woodland sleepers, Frank and I in our little nest did not agree ; but, on the contrary, woke up and had a very healthy row, the bone of contention being the division of the saddle-bags as a pillow, our one comfort that night. Poor wretches! I'm sure our most severe critics would have forgiven us for our bad tempers, if they had known how abominably uncomfortable we were. At any rate we forgave one another next morning, and by general consent the whole party was moving as soon as there was the least glimmer of dawn to guide us, and after being buffeted by the wet boughs and soaked with the chilly dew which they shook off upon us, for the space of an hour we entered upon an opening where grew the first and one of the finest pine-trees I ever saw in Svânetia.

From crest to foot the grand old forest giant was covered with long festoons of grey-beard moss, and the weight of many snowy winters had bowed him, until he looked as if he had not many more days to lord it over his neighbours. Round him and at his foot he had spread a deep thick carpet of fallen pine needles, the softest couch the forest affords, and in these, snugly ensconced between two projecting roots, some Svânetian hunter had made himself a nest, round and cosy as a bird's, sheltered from wind and rain by the boughs and roots of the old tree. Within hearing of this nest was the rush of one of the little rills that run to feed the Zesku, and here we drank long and greedily, only regretting that we had not chanced upon these good quarters the night before.

All the country hereabouts is a kind of border or debatable land, between Radcha and Svânetia. Herein no man lives and only the adventurous feed their flocks. Under almost every tall pine, from which water is not far distant, and in every mountain cave, are dead fires and blackened hearth stones, to mark the place in which cattle lifter or sportsman has passed the night. In old days no race was noted for more predatory instincts than my friends the Sváns; once or twice, so history says, they have slipped over glacier and mountain pass to lay waste the whole of the fair valley of the Rion, spoil Oni, and once even destroy Kutais, but this was long ago in the fourteenth century.

Since the time when George III. (of Georgia) was king they have done little beyond an occasional attack on Gebi, to provide themselves with wives, or a free fight with rival hunters at the drinking-places of the túr.

The encroachments of that civilisation introduced by the Russians have almost put a stop even to these little amusements, so that now there is nothing left for the restless Svân but the blood-feud and the pursuit of mountain game. It is in this latter that he spends most of his time, and if he can kill one head just over the boundary of his neighbour's domain, it is worth half a dozen killed in his own mountains.

By the banks of the Zeskuskal we sat down and breakfasted, and so likely looked the pools, and so confident were our guides of the abundance of fish in the stream at our feet, that whilst the others made a fire, I put together my rod and proceeded to whip all the likeliest places for trout.

Every kind of fly which seemed suited to the tastes of uneducated fish was tried in succession, and then two or three of Mr. Ogden's charmers for such as have reached the highest standard of piscine education. But all the temptations of Ogden, all the wiles learnt on the Gloucestershire Colne, were of no avail. Not a rise rewarded my efforts; not a single troutie, however tiny, accepted my invitation to breakfast. So we had to be content once more with our bread-and-water diet, and at eight o'clock were again moving along the river's bed.

I don't think that from the time we left Lapûr to the time we made Ushkûl there was a hundred yards level walking, except the stretch of fell just outside the latter. Frank and myself had to carry all we could, and though that was only our rifles, rugs, revolvers, and a few odds and ends, they hampered us more than the heavy loads did our men, who were used to being beasts of burden all day long. The sinewy Simon was the life of the party, jogging along light of foot and bright of eye, singing under a load that I could scarcely carry a hundred yards, over the beds of half-dry torrents, where the only marvel was that men unladen could walk with unsprained ancles along the everlasting steppingstones; through blind forest alleys, where malicious boughs caught your pack or rifle as you passed, and almost wrenched it from your back, while as soon as you were free from them, a root or bough at your feet sent you sprawling on all fours.

Turning out of the wood for a moment the track led down hill; down a hill so steep that you felt it would make you 'stand over' for the rest of your life, and up the other side at an incline that made us tremble for our back sinews. All the while we were passing through beds of tall nettles, which stung hands, neck, and face impartially.

Once during the day we stopped to dig up the roots of what, to my unbotanical eye, seemed a species of crocus, of a beautiful purple colour, which grew in profusion wherever the track was most trodden. The flowers were very large and the bulbs gregarious, if I may use such a term of flowers, growing in a thick lump of from six to sixteen together. This flower we saw once before at Shukachâlo, but nowhere else in Radcha; whereas we met with it in large quantities everywhere in Svânetia.

Once again, towards mid-day, when we had left the river's course and diverged into a region of pine-trees, amongst which already lay some sprinklings of new-fallen snow, we rested to divide a small maize loaf (our last) amongst us in a wild ravine, where a rugged grey watercourse came precipitously down to the valley from a snow peak, which almost seemed to bend over the newly-burnt pine forest round us.

It was as grim and beautiful a picture of ruin and desolation as nature ever exhibited, and the want of my lunch annoyed me far less than the want of skill in my clumsy fingers to produce some souvenir of the charred stumps, stern mountain, and rugged watercourse, with their patches of new-fallen snow.

A poor lunch is no great evil to men who have work to do; the worse it is the sooner you are ready to leave it, and the less there is of it the lighter it is to carry. So argued the philosophers in the burnt pine forest, though five minutes before I heard one of them say he would give a sovereign for a loaf of white bread.

All the afternoon we walked our level best, sometimes one, sometimes another of the least laden amongst us leading and making the running. Neither Frank nor I ever cared for walking for walking's sake, but hunger was making us wonderfully anxious to see Ushkûl.

When we first left Lapûr, now two days ago, the men had told us that with hard work we might reach Ushkûl by nightfall—at the worst we should be there by early morning of the second day. Now the light of the second day was rapidly failing, we had been going so steadily and so fast all day that the men had long since begun to complain, and yet when we asked Vassili how soon we should sight the goal of our long march, he almost broke our hearts by pointing to a new ridge of mountains just coming into sight, and saying, 'We'll camp at the foot of those to-night if possible, and to-morrow at mid-day we shall be at Ushkûl.'

After that general conversation flagged, but as, by the help of my alpenstock, I kept my place on a thread-like track along the face of a slippery grass slope, I heard frequent snatches of a soliloquy from one who was behind me : ' Bless these hills ! ' he muttered ; ' you don't catch me out of the vale again. You're no sooner down one place than you begin to go up another. Wish they were all rolled out flat and planted with "roots." Chamois and tûr! wish that fool W. had never heard of a tûr. Give me a covey of little brown birds in the corner of every field, and a little brown jug under most of the hedges ;

that's what I call sport!' And the sigh that followed this last allusion was so deep and heartfelt that it almost blew me off my precarious footing, and must have used up all the spare wind of my friend, for he never spoke again until our next halt.

There was still a little light left when we passed a resolution that we would go no further that night. We were all in too good condition to mind another two or three hours' work if there was any good to be derived from it; but, as Simon pointed out, we could not now hope to reach our journey's end before dark, and the range in front of us was covered with glaciers and new-fallen snow. The wind was blowing from the range to us, and the nearer we got to it the less we should like the keenness which the new-fallen snow would lend to the night air. So we prospected for a camp. Now this was where Frank shone. Like a certain 'grand old man,' Frank was a splendid hewer of wood, and loved the work. So while Simon, having thrown off his load, proceeded to refresh himself by standing on his head, singing and smoking by turns, Frank found two large rocks by the river, and began to chop firewood.

Simon, having let off his superfluous spirits, was asked to give his opinion on the site chosen, and at first dissented earnestly. But whilst doing so his eyes lighted on a large currant bush, covered with berries, which hung over one of the rocks, after which a gentle, contented look spread over his manly features, and he ate placidly and unceasingly for about three-quarters of an hour, till the bushes were bare, and Frank, Vassili, and I had got the worst part of the camp work done. We envied him perhaps, but we said nothing, for after all, if he did only work when he chose, when he did choose who could work like Simon?

Having crammed our bourkas into the cosiest crannies under the rocks, Simon fished out from somewhere the relics of my first chamois, and proceeded to dole out a portion to each of us. We had no bread now, nor any tea, but our ravenous hunger made the high scented old billy-goat's flesh very palatable even without salt.

By-and-bye, as we smoked a last pipe, three wild-looking figures, armed to the teeth, plodded silently out of the gloom into that part of the forest path on which the leaping flames of our log-fire cast quaint lights and shadows. As they passed they turned their faces towards the blaze, and favoured us with a searching gaze, which had not too much friendliness in it. But they never paused in their march, made no sign of having seen us save for the turning of their heads, and would have passed us without a word of salutation if they had been allowed to. But whoever they were, we did not feel inclined to let them go unhailed; so Simon and I jumped up, and leaving our weapons where they were, went out to them. They seemed a little inclined to be distrustful at first, but when they found we were honest but unfortunate hunters like themselves, they shook hands and came to our fire. They were the least civilised-looking people we had seen yet. Each of them wore a goat's skin dressed with the hair outside and the little stiff tail left on; the skin was not cut into any shape at all, but rather maintained its natural outline, and in some cases was attached to a similar one (but tailless) in front.

The effect of these rough goat-skin garments, amongst the Svâns, is very odd, and their caudal appendages, long hair, and the reed pipes on which they played, made me feel as if I had dropped in upon an evening party of satyrs.

Did I only say our guests were Svâns? If I did, allow me to apologise and present them to the reader as three of the most renowned chasseurs of Ushkûl, by name Gargi,

Georgi, and Simon, called hereafter, for distinction sake, Simon the Less. They had all been out for a Sunday shoot, and having (unluckily for us) eaten all their provisions and killed nothing were now on their way back to town, and had intended to make a night march of it, if the charms of our society had not led them out of their path.

They were not bad-looking fellows, in spite of all we had heard against their race; short men rather, with broad shoulders, and, unlike the men of Radcha, peculiar rather for their abundant hair than for their shaven pates. One of them, the leader of the three apparently, was the most marvellous likeness of our great tragic actor, in honour of whom we at once rechristened this first met of a (to us) new race.

But little Simon was the man who interested us most, for after a few inquiries our Simon discovered that the little man was the son of the great bear-slayer of Ushkúl, of whose prowess we had already heard more than once. On asking him how many bears the old man really had killed, he said that his father had kept count up to one hundred and twenty-five, but that since then he had lost count, and his son said he didn't think he had killed more than three or four lately. Our informant had himself added twenty-seven to the collection of off forepaws which adorned the paternal mansion.

By-and-bye our guests grew sleepy, but with characteristic caution they would not lie down by our fire, preferring rather to build one of their own a couple of dozen yards off, where, though near enough for conversational purposes, they could still keep together, and have an eye on the strangers. In spite of his friendly manner towards them a few whispered words of my old hunter's before I turned in convinced me that the Radcha men were just as suspicious of the Sváns as the Sváns were of us; and, indeed, wherever we went with Simon and Vassili afterwards, we could always see that, though civil and even friendly, there was a kind of uneasiness in their intercourse such as might exist between a cat and a fox terrier on the same hearthrug, who, though at peace for the moment, felt keenly that it was not their normal condition.

Poor old Simon! The term of his service had nearly expired now, and he was very determined to see that we left his hands safe and sound. Twice I opened my eyes during the night. The first time he was still crouching over the fire, his pipe in his mouth, and at the other fire were three figures also sitting up. But Simon had his eye on them.

When next I woke, I felt someone touch me, and without stirring I opened my eyes and saw my good fellow, having kicked the logs together and added fresh ones, take off his own blanket and tuck it carefully round me, and then with a shiver crouch into his own few rags and curl himself up like a faithful watch dog at my feet. Of course, as soon as I thought he slept I returned the loan, but when I woke I was rolled up in it again.

I was very sorry to lose Simon; for, though he would always smoke when he ought not to (and indeed when he ought to as well, if there is such a time), though he would waste hours eating quantities of fruit which would have given any three other men cholera, and making scores of reed pipes, out of none of which he ever got a tune, he was for all that so bright-tempered, so honest, light-hearted, so enormously strong, so capable of enduring prolonged abstinence and fatigue, so kindly and quick to see what you wanted, and to supply the want, that I am bound to say, in looking back, I regard him as the best fellow I ever met in the Caucasus. Vassili, Frank's servant, though not so strong or clever as Simon, was an honest, merry rascal, and perhaps in camp a harder worker than my man.

Altogether, I agree in what Simon and his *confrères* used to say, that Radcha men are the best men in this part of the Caucasus, theft is unknown amongst them they say, and I never heard of their being particularly addicted to any other vices. Certainly, as we crossed out of the border-land into Svânetia proper on the morrow, we felt we should be lucky if we found as good and genial a governor or as well-ordered a province as those we left behind in Baron Geikin and Radcha.

As soon as it was light we were all up, and anxious to be off. As we had not seen a village since we left Gebi a fortnight ago, and Ushkûl was reported to be almost (if not quite) the largest village in Svânetia, we hoped for great things on our arrival there. Of course there had been rain in the valley and more snow on the mountain in the night, thanks to which the jungles of angelica, through which our path lay, were like a perpetual shower-bath; and the early morning breeze off the snow did not help to bring a glow into our limbs after our involuntary tub. To do the snow justice it had made Davâchora, as the men called the mountain ahead of us, the prettiest picture in black and white I ever saw; but I think if we had had any breakfast, even the tiniest crust, we should have enjoyed the bold outlines and delicate snow traceries of the mountain better.

About nine o'clock we got to the end of the valley we had followed so long, and another horrible series of hills to climb frowned down at us from the other side of a fairly deep and rapid stream. I think someone, old Simon probably, tucked Frank's thirteen or fourteen stone of beef and bone under his arm and carried him across dryshod. If he did not do so on this occasion he had often done it before.

As for myself, I was so wretchedly wet already that a little water more or less didn't matter, so not even taking the trouble to jump from one high stone to another, I plunged sulkily in and plodded sullenly away on the other side as if a wetting to the waist was all in the day's work, and didn't so much matter when one was once in for being 'jolly miserable.'

Frank and the men seemed much of the same mind, and we all plodded along as if we were on a treadmill, without talking or pausing much until we gained the top of a high bluff about 11 A.M., from which the men told us the rest of the road lay over smooth downs, and the incline, if any, was down hill. Then our spirits rose.

Some one said there was an iron spring about a mile off, so we gave Simon the Less twenty-five kopecks to go and bring us a skinful of the water, and on this and a pipe we breakfasted. Meanwhile, in our trusting innocence we sent on one of the Svâns with the bearskins to secure us a room in the village, and have some bread ready and a few fowls cooked by the time we arrived. Then we rested for an hour, after which we showed those Svâns and the men of Radcha how to walk on the flat.

Frank's spirits certainly went up as the road went down, and the way he strode over those downs and the snatches of song he sang are things which true men of Radcha will never forget. But the appetite engendered by early rising, hard exercise, and a breakfast of iron water and tobacco smoke was becoming extremely painful.

Before long, too, we came upon our three avant-couriers calmly seated on a knoll by a spring waiting for us to come up with them. They had thought matters over, and come to the conclusion that it would be plenty of time to order breakfast when we got to Ushkúl.

It wasn't a bit of good swearing at them, but I'm afraid it was just one of those moments when a good candid expression of your opinion of your fellow man is not only a luxury but a necessity. Again we sent the men on ahead, or at least one of them—the fellow with the lightest load—but it was no good. After going some distance he threw down the bearskins which he was carrying, and said we might carry them ourselves; after which he sat down by the wayside and scowled and laughed at us by turns. So far the people of Svânetia had not impressed us favourably.

By-and-bye we saw far up on the rising ground to our right a couple of fellows with some cattle, and another making hay-cocks almost on the summit of the ridge. A loud 'cooey' from our guides brought an answer from the hill-tops, and then in wonderfully clear shrill tones they explained that if the people above had any bread, those down below had money, and would pay for it. Whether they could distinguish what was said is a question, but they soon came bounding down to us, and from their bashliks we disinterred our first loaves of Svânetian bread.

Conceive a thing like a large Sally Lunn, only flatter, made of a mixture of the coarsest oatmeal and sand, very heavy, more than half sour, and very wet. When you have imagined this, you have imagined the thing which the unsophisticated Svân looks upon as the staff of life. Still, bad as it was, only one of our party refused to eat of it, and that one our interpreter Platon. At first I was very angry with him, considering that as he had been bred in the country, what was good enough for us ought to be good enough for him. But he was right for all that, as our disordered digestions and a violent attack of heartburn told us next morning. To eat of the bread of Svânetia with impunity, even an ostrich would require to be nourished on it from earliest infancy, otherwise it would assuredly be too much even for his digestion.

It was about half an hour after this light and wholesome meal, that we saw down below us two black towers on the top of a low round hill, grim-looking and ruined, like the outworks of some fortified place long since given up to fire and the sword. 'There is Mookmer!' said one of the guides. 'Mookmer, hang Mookmer!' we answered; 'where is Ushkûl?' 'Ushkûl is Mookmer,' explained our guide, and gradually we learnt that the towers before us were on the outskirts of a collection of three hamlets, the collective name for which was Mookmer, the most important amongst them being Ushkûl.

But Ushkûl is so unique, so unlike any other town or village I ever saw, so extremely unlike any that I ever wish to see again, that I must give it a chapter to itself, hoping that the journey thither has not been as weary for my readers as it was for us. Yet even for us these weary tramps were not altogether wasted; for if they taught nothing else, they taught me some sympathy with my horse—a sympathy born of suffering; and, I hope, whenever I remember our walk thither, I shall not forget to spare my poor mount at the start, in order that he may be able to boil up a gallop at the finish.

www.ingramcontent.com/pod-product-compliance
Lightning Source LLC
Chambersburg PA
CBHW032059220426
43664CB00008B/1066